The New Flooring Idea Book

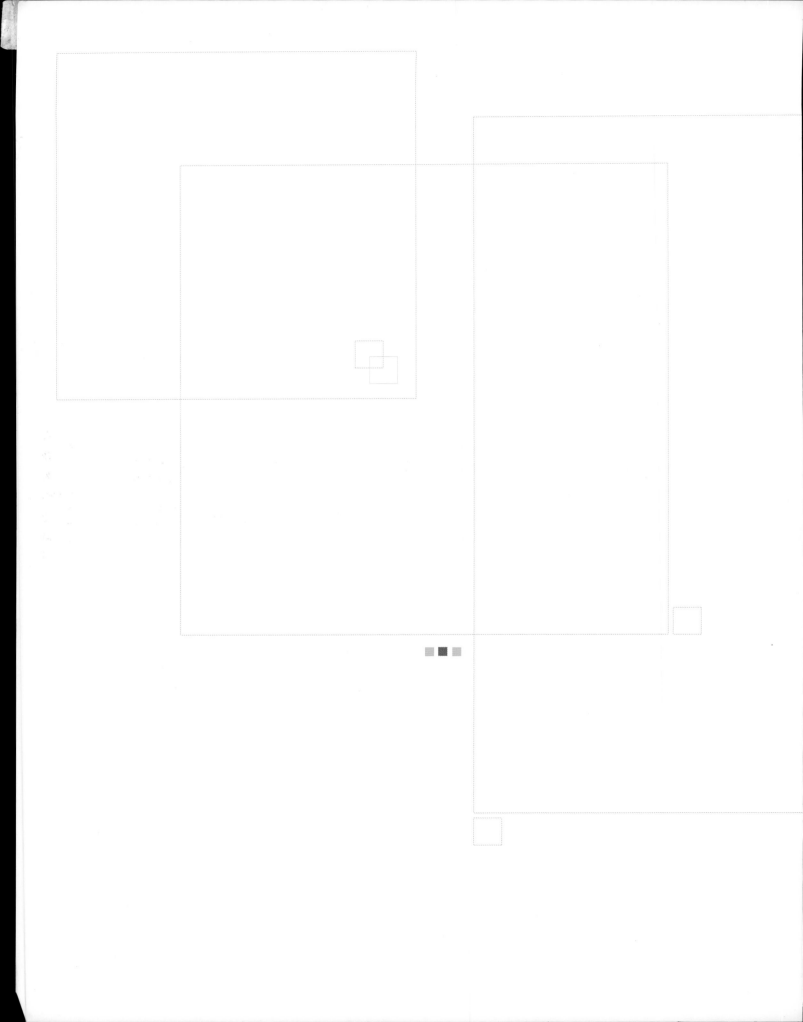

The New Flooring Idea Book

Creating Style from the Ground Up

Regina Cole

GLOUCESTER MASSACHUSETTS

ROCKPORT
PUBLISHERS

First published in the United States of America by
Rockport Publishers, Inc.
33 Commercial Street
Gloucester, Massachusetts 01930-5089
Telephone: (978) 282-9590
Facsimile: (978) 283-2742
www.rockpub.com

ISBN: 1-56496-731-X
10 9 8 7 6 5 4 3 2 1
Page Design: madison design & advertising, inc.
Front Cover: Graham Atkins-Hughes/Red Cover (main image);
    Bruce Martin (top); Lanny Provo (middle and bottom)
Back Cover: Winfried Heinze/Red Cover (left);
    Scott Dorrance (right)
Printed in China.

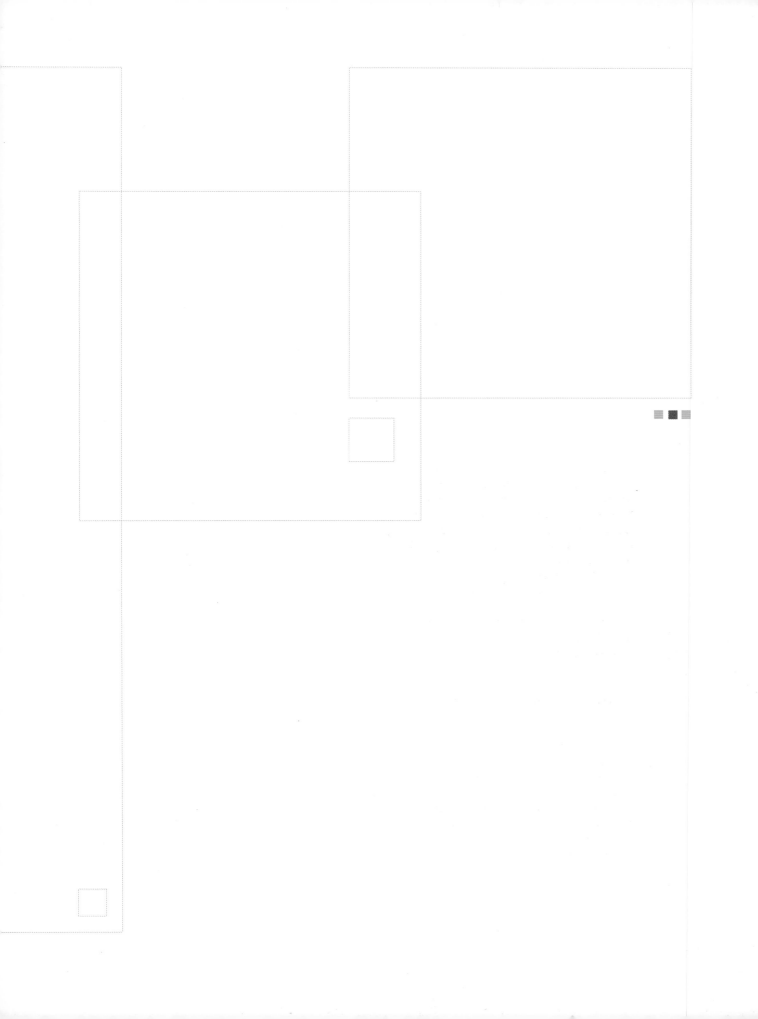

The New
Flooring Idea Book
Creating Style from the Ground Up

Contents

Introduction

Flooring Predates Houses

Before our early ancestors built shelters, they very likely softened their primitive caves with sweet grasses, warm animal skins, and clean sand. Such materials provided practical aids to comfort and cleanliness, as well as aesthetic and tactile pleasure.

Flooring still performs the same functions. As far as we've come in the vast world of house construction and design, we still want our floors to feel good and look great. If, in addition, they dampen sound, smell good, reflect light, age beautifully, or make it easier to keep the room clean, all the better.

That's the beauty of flooring: One of the most basic and functional components of a house provides an astonishing variety of decorative choices. There are few materials that someone hasn't tried to put on a floor at some point; some as unexpected as glass, metal, bamboo, or leather are surprisingly successful in the modern home. The familiar standbys such as wood and ceramic tile have benefited from technological improvements that make them easier to install and maintain, more affordable, and available in a greater variety. If you think you know flooring, look again; advances in manufacturing processes and in the development of bonding and finishing materials have made some of the most familiar old flooring brand new. A common complaint in the housing world is: "They don't make it like they used to." In flooring, the opposite is true: Before now, they didn't even make a lot of what is available to us today.

Whether you are building a new house, adding to your present home, or refurbishing a room, emulate those ancestral cave dwellers. In other words, install flooring for comfort, cleanliness, and aesthetic and tactile pleasure. Don't be afraid to indulge your cravings for luxury or beauty or progressive design. The floor, as the largest horizontal surface in a room, is vitally important to a unified design scheme. One definition of "floor" is "a surface as a foundation." When you think about the elements of function, comfort, and beauty that are so important in your home, think flooring. The foundation of a room is a logical place to start when you are developing an overall design scheme.

After all, you can't have rooms without floors, so have the flooring you want. So much is available, at so many price points, that it's easy to feel overwhelmed. Use this book to help guide your decision-making process. Take advantage of the information we've compiled about the variety of choices in today's marketplace while relying on your own likes, dislikes, and functional requirements. If you learn all you can while trusting your own instincts and taste, the result is bound to be flooring that works well, looks good, and is uniquely suited to you and your home.

Choosing the right floor can be either the first or the final step in creating a great room, whether you are designing a new home from scratch, renovating an old beauty, or simply updating the look of an existing room. Flooring choices are as varied as those for furnishings, window treatments, and wall coverings—so how do you choose what to put underfoot?

Section 1
Working Out a Game Plan

Working Out a
Game Plan

Think for a moment about fashion. Imagine the most spectacular, glamorous ensemble that you can conjure up. Now, finish that outfit off with a pair of dowdy or simply inappropriate shoes. That's how important picking out the right floor is to finish—indeed, even to serve as the foundation for—a beautifully designed room.

Just as a pair of shoes can make or break an outfit, the right floor is integral to holding together the design and décor of any space. No matter how attractive a room, or how carefully chosen its furnishings, it will not shine unless the floor—or floor covering—is as breathtaking as the space that surrounds it. And just as fashion designers are continually creating, re-creating, and reinventing footwear for the shoe-obsessed, home designers are continually introducing new materials, styles, and colors of flooring, and in doing so, are reinventing home design.

Imagine a bathroom decked in dark pieces of slate, accented with sparkling glass, or a kitchen outfitted with thick planks of solid cherry. These might be a far cry from the tile or linoleum that typically cover these spaces, but remember, you don't have to be conventional to have a floor that works in a room. A floor is about more than having something to walk on. It's about understanding and working with different materials and deciding what they convey to you and to anyone who enters your home. New flooring is about building style in a room, from the ground up. ■■■

New and classic: the beauty of wood in an ecofriendly look-alike.

Use laminates for color and high-traffic areas.

Consider the Options

While natural hardwoods, stunning tiles, and luxurious carpets are among the most popular options, old-fashioned treatments such as classic linoleum and rich, supple leather are resurfacing in both modern and renovated homes. New alternatives, including laminate flooring and custom-tinted concrete, merge style with practicality to stunning effect. And a bevy of new flooring materials derived from renewable—even recycled—materials offers ecofriendly and uniquely beautiful alternatives to old-fashioned floors.

Streamline your choice by remembering that your floor is about more than appearance. Consider the way a floor plays to most of your senses: sight (the color, look, and light-reflecting qualities); sound (how it affects the room's acoustics); touch (cold or warm underfoot, hard or soft); and even scent (the subtle aromas of leather and linoleum, the way rugs can trap odors). Think not only about the style of the room but the practical requirements: A high-traffic vestibule requires something durable, while a cozy family room benefits from the warmth and sound-absorbing qualities of wall-to-wall carpeting.

New Floor/Old House

Working with What You Have

Installing new flooring in your old house is an opportunity to introduce style that's fresh, new, and tailored to today's lifestyle, while taking advantage of the quality construction that is the hallmark of many old houses. When you explore the options in today's flooring world, you may learn to see your old house in a new way. New flooring can serve to highlight the character and charm that first attracted you to your house.

Highlight What Works; Help for What Doesn't

Small, cramped rooms, for example, can be visually enlarged with beige wall-to-wall carpeting. Choose a beige with yellow undertones to bring warmth into the décor; if you want a cool effect, choose a gray beige. If you would like to emphasize the warm tones in old woodwork, lay carpets or install resilient flooring in saturated reds and greens that bring out the colors of mahogany or oak. Rooms in your old house may have good proportions that have gotten lost in fussy or unfocused decorative schemes; here is a chance to show off their "good bones." Stencil or paint the floor in geometric or border patterns, install pale stone tiles, or lay one of the new neutral-colored sisal carpets that are bound with a contrasting cotton border. Chose a size and shape that follows the outline of the room, leaving a 1- or 2-foot (.3- or .6-meter) perimeter of bare floor. The border color can echo wall or upholstery colors or it can strike a dramatic note in a neutral room.

Use new flooring to emphasize what's best in a room, whether built-ins, a wonderful view, beautiful woodwork, or good furniture. A superb collection of antique furniture can be showcased to great effect against a backdrop of cutting-edge flooring. Imagine the impact of gilded Louis XVI chairs on a floor of glass tiles or a curvaceous Rococo Revival parlor suite with red plush upholstery arranged on flat gray wool wall-to-wall carpet. One effective way of calling attention to a particular piece is to place an area rug under it; one well-known example is the style icon of a rocking chair on a braided rug. A jewel-toned prayer rug could serve as a frame for a glass and steel coffee table. Put your leather and rosewood Eames recliner and ottoman on a deep shaggy rug in white or cream. Emphasize the pure lines of a Shaker table by placing it on dark gray slate. In each instance, the impact of each piece is heightened by the choice of flooring or floor covering.

Consider Your Old Floors a Plus

Chances are good that they are structurally sound; well-built floors can be the basis for a new look without great expense. A common scenario for the new owners of an old house is to rip up worn-out resilient flooring, only to find a crude, unfinished wood surface that requires some sort of covering. Consider some of today's decorative paint products, which can provide surprising texture and color. For instance, you might apply two contrasting colors of supremely tough paint, then "comb."

Historic character and charm are highlighted with a new wood laminate floor in a dark chestnut color. These modern floors can "float" over the surface of existing flooring.

Historically, it was not unusual to install new hardwood over an existing softwood floor; in this case, the old floor became part of the subfloor. Many of today's flooring options (vinyl sheet or tiles and "floating" floors, to name only two) can be installed over existing flooring. Use manufacturers' guidelines when you lay one material over another. Cork floors, for instance, should not be installed over linoleum, vinyl, or rubber since the materials experience such different rates of expansion and contraction. Once you've ascertained the compatability of the different materials, the primary thing to keep in mind is the thickness added by each new layer. Doors should swing without touching the floor; baseboards and wall elements should not be compromised. Also, remember the overall proportions of your room. A mere inch can make the difference between pleasing proportions and an awkward fit in some rooms. Since many of today's laminates, vinyl floor tiles, and resilient sheet-flooring varieties are newly slender, many more options are at your disposal than in the past. Even ceramic tile and stone flooring are thinner today.

When to Start Over

When should you go through the (not inconsiderable) effort of ripping up existing flooring? Keep in mind that all flooring problems do not mandate a new floor: Rough, stained, discolored, blemished, burned, or gouged wood floors can usually be cured by refinishing. Squeaks, probably at the top of the list of reasons why people want new floors, can be isolated and silenced. Even more serious old-floor problems are fixable. A wood floor may have been sanded and refinished too many times, causing planks or strips to break down, especially along the edges. Deep scratches or dents may mar the surface and present safety hazards. Old resilient flooring may have worn through to the subfloor or underlayment; tiles may be cracked, grout deteriorating. As distressing as these problems are, repairs can usually be made. Experts on the subject of old houses advise that most old floors stand a greater chance of remaining stable if they are not disturbed. If you are not sure whether you should work with what you have, contact a qualified house inspector. He or she can assess the structural soundness of your floors and can often counsel you in the best ways to address problems.

Paint is one of the most effective and least costly ways to refresh the appearance of an old floor. For a less traditional effect, consider faux finishes or trompe l'oeil.

STILL THE SQUEAKS AND CREAKS

IN MOST CASES, A CREAKING FLOOR IS CAUSED BY LOOSENING OF THE NAILS HOLDING THE SUBFLOOR TO THE JOISTS. IF THE CREAK IS IN AN EXPOSED SUB-FLOOR, AS IN A BASEMENT, DRIVE A SMALL WEDGE BETWEEN THE JOIST AND THE LOOSE BOARD ABOVE IT. IF IT IS IMPOSSIBLE TO REACH THE SUBFLOOR, LOCATE THE JOIST BY TAPPING ON THE FLOOR, THEN DRIVE 2- OR 3-INCH (5 OR 8 CM) FINISHING NAILS THROUGH THE FLOOR, SUBFLOOR, AND INTO THE JOIST. USE A NAIL SET TO DRIVE THE NAIL BELOW THE SURFACE OF THE WOOD SO THAT YOU DON'T HIT THE FINISHED FLOOR WITH THE HAMMER AND MAR THE FINISH. THEN FILL THE HOLE WITH PUTTY OR STAIN THAT MATCHES THE FLOOR.

IF A LOOSE BOARD IS THE CAUSE, YOU CAN LOCATE THE BOARD BY ITS MOVEMENT WHEN WEIGHT IS PUT ON IT. USE 2-INCH (5 CM) FINISHING NAILS, DRIVEN AT AN ANGLE, TO FASTEN IT. THEN USE THE NAIL SET.

A new kitchen in an old house called for a compatible floor; in this case, honey-toned knotty pine echoes the rustic old post-and-beam construction.

Troubleshooting: Framing and Structure

There are deeper, hidden reasons for floor troubles, and sometimes an old floor is simply beyond help. Perhaps your house had a persistent leak: If water worked its way in and caused rot, then the floor will have to be replaced. Defective framing can cause sagging and sloping floors. Floor joists that are too small or inadequately supported can also be the reason for uneven floor wear. (If this is the case in a house you are considering for purchase, keep in mind the truism that poor carpentry in one area is a tip-off to substandard construction throughout the house.) Floors that have been exposed to water may warp or bulge upwards. Wide cracks between floorboards are a sign of poor workmanship or of shrinkage caused by wood that was improperly dried or not stored correctly at the time of installation. Or perhaps the subfloor suffered damage, in which case, the whole section must be replaced to the nearest joist.

New structural beams can be "sistered" to the old. In this process, failing old weight-bearing elements are not removed but rather attached to strong new ones. If space does not allow this, new steel beams or columns provide optimum strength.

If you do install a new floor in an old house, choose what harmonizes with the interior's overall design scheme. If the house is architecturally important, extremely old, or a great example of a specific decorative style, you will probably choose to reproduce the original flooring. In most cases, however, the options are only limited by your taste and budget.

Starting Fresh
Build in Your Choices from the Start

Few things are more thrilling than planning a new home of your own. This is the opportunity to define your preferences and to act on them, thus creating a living space that is uniquely yours. Flooring is a crucial element in beautiful décor: Think floors when you first consider your home's style. Include your flooring choices in the plan from the beginning to avoid costly and disruptive changes later on and create a decorative scheme that is a stylistic whole.

Some flooring can be laid directly over a cement slab. Terrazzo, ceramic tile, and concrete are a few examples that require no additional subflooring between those materials and even incorporate cement in the installation process. Whatever the material of your subfloor, now is the time to work out issues of compatibility. In new construction, your only concern is apt to be the differential rates of expansion and contraction between the subfloor and the finish flooring. With forethought, these concerns can be minimized or even eliminated.

Advance planning will determine color schemes and assure that materials are ordered in sufficient quantities. If, for instance, your floors are intended to tone from lighter to darker as you walk deeper into your house, this is the time to assure that it will happen just the way you want—long before unmatched flooring meets an expensive construction crew.

Think about all your flooring issues and you'll be ahead of the game. You'll want to give primary consideration to your likes and dislikes, but don't stop at aesthetics. Think about whether you like the work of maintenance associated with some types of flooring or whether you are the no-muss, no-fuss type. How important is noise? Does your definition of luxury include sinking into deep pile with every step? And then there's longevity: Are you willing to pay more for a floor that will last longer? Some kinds of flooring show the dirt more readily than others; professionals must install some. Does anyone in the home have needs that mandate particular features? Examples might be nonslip walking surfaces for elderly or visually-impaired family members or easy-to-clean floors in a household populated by children and pets.

A carefully planned work alcove under the stairs gains design coherence from a neutral floor that continues up the stair treads.

Start with Style

Start with a clear sense of the house's style. Whether it is formal, casual, traditional, modern, country, or urban will dictate its design vocabulary, including the flooring. Decide what you want the flooring to do, other than to provide a surface to walk on. This might include dampening sound, calling attention to a particular area, providing a backdrop for a collection of rugs, or showcasing a beautiful local material such as wood or stone.

Is a compatible combination of bright colors your personal bliss? White walls and simple design make way for color exploding up from the floor.

You may wish to play up the drama of a broad expanse of space or create intimate conversation areas. If you include flooring in your design plans, rooms will come together more gracefully.

This is a great time for list making. Write down what matters to you, what you need, what you want—and enjoy!

Timing is Everything

Some kinds of flooring, concrete and stone among them (above), are most easily installed while the house is under construction. Pouring and curing concrete, hauling heavy stone, troweling, clomping about in caked work boots—these are not done comfortably near finished surfaces. It's also better for your health to avoid heavy-construction sites (and to take appropriate protective measures, such as wearing masks and respirators, when doing it yourself). Other types of flooring, such as hardwood, should not be laid until the room is further along in structure and finish. Laminate floors can even be laid in a room that's more or less furnished. Leather flooring requires a week's acclimation, during which time you can't use the room. So, think ahead and plan your new floor construction for your own comfort and convenience.

The Floor and
Design Implications

Deciding on the right floor for a particular room is not about taste alone. You have to consider the size and shape of the room, its architecture, furnishings, style, the amount and quality of natural light, and the room's purpose. Once all these elements have been carefully weighed, you can consider the different materials that might work in a room, and the way each of your options can provide a multitude of different results.

When you begin your flooring process, plan (for new construction) or determine (if already established) a room's overall use, appearance, and personality.

This quality is sometimes hard to pinpoint, since personality (in homes as well as in people) comes together from so many intangible and subtle elements. If your home is a strong example of a specific architectural style, or a combination of styles, your decorating efforts will be easiest and most successful if you know what it is and follow its directions. You may choose a design scheme that is not customary for the house's architecture, just as you might dress in a surprisingly unconventional way, but if this is done without knowledge and intent, the result is rarely flattering.

Architecture and Flooring: A Marriage of Style

Architecture provides the style definition. Look to the moldings, window openings, base-boards, mantelpieces, and other architectural elements (or lack thereof) to determine whether the space is formal, classical, modern, or rustic. In older houses, especially, these will mirror the house's exterior style elements. General characteristics can be further narrowed down to a definition of the house's individual style. This is often a reflection of the popular tastes of the time at which the house was built. Often (though certainly not always) a shortcut to deter-mining house style is to know the date of construction, and then to match it to interior and exterior design elements. But if you can't exactly pinpoint your home's age or style, don't worry. Many older houses were added to over time, thus changing or diluting their original stylistic statements. In recent decades, houses were often built with design elements bor-rowed from a number of sources, pared down, or reinvented.

A stylish flooring personality may be hard to define, but it is unmistakable when seen. Here, materials are mixed in surprising ways for effective and practical traffic flow.

As you study the details that make up your house's stylistic whole, you will come to recognize it as formal or informal, plain or highly ornamented, casual, urban, minimalist, romantic, country, or eclectic. In other words, you will get to know your house's design statement, even if that can't be pigeonholed into one recognizable style definition.

The Right Floor for the Room

Once you have determined your house's style and whether you will create a stylistic whole or 'work against type,' your first question is use. Form really does follow function, and your room will work best if you install the floor that is best for its intended use. An obvious example of this is the fact that vinyl, stone, or ceramic tiles, not inlaid wood or antique Oriental rugs, are popular in bathrooms.

The first experience of a floor is tactile. Your mind registers a soft rug, hard marble, or creaky wood, and your initial preference will be biased for a floor that is hard or soft. The

Dare to work against type—a sisal carpet instead of the traditional pine boards or hooked rugs emphasized the furniture in a country bedroom while suffusing the whole scheme with calm and warmth.

room's use, of course, will help you make this determination. Visual cues can effectively underscore this message. The flooring surface establishes the primary horizontal plane in a room and underlies the entire design scheme you want to communicate. Gray wall-to-wall carpeting, for instance, unifies space, whereas scattered Oriental rugs establish distinct walking and seating patterns, as do stenciling, inlay, borders, or center medallions. Give some thought to the subtle messages communicated by materials: Leather floor tiles hint at the atmosphere of libraries or of comfortable retreats; bamboo speaks of the Far East; dark gray slate evokes the severe beauty of northern winters.

Think about the effects of reflected light. Very shiny floors look cold; matte flooring gives the appearance of softness. The way light plays off the grain or wood or the surface striations in stone is part of their beauty; use these materials to highlight these characteristics.

Mood is set by color. Brown may be the color that comes to mind when you think of a wood floor, but it is just the beginning of a range of colorful possibilities. Likewise, ceramic tile is often laid in a monochromatic earth-toned or checkerboard two-tone scheme, but tiles are so colorful that you can have a rainbow on your floor today. In fact, you are not limited to conventional effects, as most kinds of flooring are now available in great color ranges.

Style is personality. Underlying a furniture arrangement of simple elegance and saturated color is classic, unadorned flooring.

Take advantage of the choices for mood-altering design impact. Light-colored floors will make a room appear larger, while dark floors promote an intimate atmosphere. Texture, too, contributes to the mood; a smooth, unbroken surface feels streamlined. A mixture of materials gives the impression of depth and complexity. Natural materials in earth tones can appear to bring the outdoors in. For a modern look, use pale neutral floor colors to give the room a clean, uncluttered appearance.

A pale wood floor, painted and stenciled, forms the base for the dreamy, tranquil aesthetic of a seaside home. Flooring colors, carefully matched in the décor, echo the outdoors.

Color and Pattern

If your floor is tiled, carpeted, stenciled, or painted, choose an overall pattern that is consistent with the room's other decorative elements in color, formality, architectural style, and drama. The size of a pattern is important, but scale is even more important. Generally, small patterns work best in small rooms, and large patterns in large rooms—but don't underestimate the dramatic possibilities of large patterns in small rooms. Just make sure that the scale of the pattern is consistent with your overall design statement. For example, in a small room with hefty architectural elements such as boldly scaled moldings or a massive overmantel, scale the floor patterns to those elements, not to the size of the room. Keep the rest of the décor simple to achieve this successfully; otherwise, you are apt to create visually claustrophobic clutter. A small, modern room grows when pale, neutral-colored furnishings rest against a bold, overscaled pattern on the floor.

Use carpeting to create a pattern. Lay area rugs to lead the eye toward a focal point or a distant view.

Pattern can be a thorny issue in today's interior designs. Use what works for you, and if you keep your home's innate personality in mind, you won't go wrong.

Furniture placement determines how we move through a room. Flooring is the best way to establish sections of specific use, whether with area rugs, or by laying flooring in pathways and seating areas. For example, place a carpet under the dining room table or outline the area under it with a different color of the same material. To correct a difficult-to-follow layout, continue the tiles from the entry to the living room threshold, or toward the stairs. Your kitchen floor might be surfaced in hard-wearing vinyl tile, with a breakfast nook or seating area defined with a different color tile or outlined with a border. Moving from hard to soft flooring is an excellent way to signal use areas; for example, when the wood floor of a hallway is broken with an area rug under a telephone table and chair.

Dark flooring, here in stained concrete, promotes intimacy, something used to great effect in a colorful, lighthearted breakfast nook.

New Shortcuts to Flooring Personality

Aluminum, stainless steel, and zinc floors speak of a sophisticated, urban aesthetic. Decorators often use this hard-edged statement to punctuate other flooring, especially in spacious lofts. Metal flooring can be particularly effective when used to define traffic paths, use areas, and staircases in vast, open spaces or to evoke the atmosphere of a Soho loft in an otherwise traditional building. Another cutting-edge look increasingly found in today's architecturally designed interiors is that of stained concrete. Both metal and concrete can be softened without compromise to their industrial look with area carpets that have an exaggerated depth of pile in the new paper, natural fiber, or synthetic designs. Computer-printed carpeting in high-tech-derived images sends an unmistakably modern message. Or, to create an avant-garde atmosphere steeped in subtlety, think of sisal or flat-woven worsted wool carpeting installed wall-to-wall in shades of taupe or mushroom.

Modern Looks

Other materials appropriate to sleek, luxurious modernism are polished stone, rubber, neutral wall-to-wall carpeting, or a sophisticated vinyl. For the unmistakable look of the Moderne period, use cork flooring in rectangular patterns, perhaps with a border or use terrazzo in

period-appropriate designs and colors. Update the look by choosing tertiary colors in vogue today—warm taupes, grayed blacks and whites, yellowed greens, smoky blues and purples, and dusty pinks and peaches.

Sleek, luxurious modernism is expressed in highly polished stone. Shades of black and gray provide pattern and sophistication.

Classic Looks

Thin stone and wood parquet flooring tiles, backed with easy-to-install mesh, are the modern shortcut to refined, classic interiors rich with moldings, silk draperies, antique furniture, and fine art. In these types of rooms, areas are defined with Aubusson rugs or Persian carpets.

Country Looks

At the folksy end of the design spectrum is the Southwestern or Spanish Colonial room, with its massive ceiling beams and rough plaster walls. Here, terra-cotta Mexican tile or honed stone pavers are an important part of establishing a well-loved rural design personality. Heighten the level of interest of this look with wood: Wood laminates and engineered flooring allow the use of mixed materials without the expensive and time-consuming custom work required in the past.

A country farmhouse interior is best evoked with wide pine boards, complete with knots and other surface imperfections. Fortunately, you can get this look without having to spend a few generations achieving it; you can find it in today's engineered floors, in reused old flooring, and in laminates. Wood floors can be painted, stenciled, bleached, or left untreated and scattered with hooked, braided, or woven area rugs. Flooring, like the rest of the house, is unpretentious, simple, and colorful. Another charming flooring choice for this kind of décor is linoleum, especially in the retro colors and patterns that recall kitchens of the first part of the twentieth century.

Arts and Crafts homes feature flooring that seeks to bring nature indoors and to echo the house's natural surroundings. Local wood or stone, accented with tribal rugs, underscores the handcrafted elements of these homes. Achieve this atmosphere with a recently introduced hardwood flooring type, in which richly colored and patterned oak varieties are bonded together into wide pieces of uniform length. Finger-joining, as this is called, is also available in engineered flooring and it creates a handmade flooring look with unprecedented ease of installation.

Bamboo flooring creates subtle patterns and echoes similar hues in the sand of a faraway beach.

A CYBER STROLL THROUGH THE WORLD OF FLOORING

HOW DO YOU SEE VAST REALMS OF FLOORING WITHOUT SPENDING YEARS ON YOUR FEET? YOU PROBABLY ALREADY LOOK AT PICTURES IN BOOKS AND MAGAZINES. NOW GET ON-LINE: AN EVER-INCREASING NUMBER OF MANUFACTURERS POST THEIR PRODUCTS ON THE INTERNET. THE BEST SITES FEATURE LUSH PHOTOGRAPHY, DETAILED SPECIFICATIONS, ANSWERS TO FREQUENTLY ASKED QUESTIONS, AND INSTALLATION TIPS. GO THERE, AS WELL, FOR INFORMATION FROM TRADE ORGANIZATIONS, ON-LINE RETAIL STORES, AND THE OFTEN-INVALUABLE INPUT FROM OTHER CONSUMERS. ELECTRONIC BROWSING CAN LEAD YOU TO THE BEST FLOORING STORES AND FLOORING DEPARTMENTS OF HOME-DESIGN STORES AND TO PRODUCTS YOU MAY NOT HAVE KNOWN ABOUT. THEN, WHEN YOU ACTUALLY STRIKE OUT TO SEE, FEEL, SMELL, AND TOUCH THE FLOORING THAT INTERESTS YOU, YOUR SEARCH WILL BE FAR MORE STREAMLINED AND PURPOSEFUL, AND FAR MORE REWARDING.

Floor
Issues

The way your floor looks is important, but so is the way it sounds, feels, smells, how much it costs, whether it's easy to care for, and how long it can be expected to last. Each material has intrinsic characteristics that affect performance. Learn about these characteristics before you buy and install and you will get the kind of floor that is best for you in the long run. Remember that characteristics of noise and discomfort are exaggerated over time. What is slightly inconvenient or irritating now will most likely drive you crazy later.

To ascertain your own personal flooring issues, make a list of general qualities and characteristics of a home that are important to you. You may never have associated some of these with flooring, but write them down anyway. You probably know whether you find dark rooms depressing; be aware that some kinds of flooring absorb (instead of reflect) light. Some people value tactile qualities above others, some have great sensitivity to sound. Whatever consistently pleases or displeases you should go on your list. For some, it is very important that the materials in their home come from nature. There are people for whom the way a thing or place looks is always the most important aspect; for others, aesthetics are always secondary to cost considerations. If you hate dirt, write it down. This is the place to list aversions and positive associations. Perhaps you have unhappy memories of a particular kind of floor; you won't want to inadvertently re-create it in your home. Does cork remind you of the 1950s décor of your favorite aunt? Write it down. Maybe the smell of linoleum recalls a happy childhood. Your list is uniquely your own and it will help you to remember what you want if the flooring sales staff is giving you the hard sell. ■ ■ ■

Brick is time-honored flooring in an entry. Brick is not dirt-sensitive, will absorb and hold solar heat from the windows above, and it signals informality and transition from the outside.

Aesthetics

No matter how "perfect" a particular type of flooring material may be for its intended use, if you don't like it, it's not right for you. You may feel pressured by considerations of cost, practicality, historic precedent, or momentary fashion, but you are the one who will live with the flooring installed in your home. Choose what appeals to you. There are so many flooring options available today that you should not have to settle for anything you don't want to see every day. Even if one material is presented to you as "the only thing that will do," there is usually at least one acceptable substitute. Today's superb cutting, milling, and bonding technologies have created new permutations in almost all flooring materials. They can be made to look or act like something entirely different from what they started out as, with little or no compromise in quality. Know what you are working with in terms of architectural style, intended use, personality, and price range. Then, follow your heart.

Solid hardwood flooring is the gold standard for deeply traditional interiors. It is beautiful but expensive.

Cost

The cost of a floor is often greater than simply the cost of the material. In a showroom, the per-square-foot cost given for each type of flooring does not include the cost of labor. Depending on the installation process, this can be a little or a whole lot.

An example is the great range of prices associated with the various types of wood floors. Laminate wood flooring is appropriate for do-it-yourselfers and is manufactured to resemble a number of wood species. It can be installed with no labor cost except for your own time. Except for a possible foam underlayment, it may not require any additional tools or materials. Laminate flooring can be priced quite reasonably. Solid hardwood flooring is at the other end of the cost spectrum. Oak, maple, and beech are expensive, and installing the strips or planks is time-consuming and demands a level of skill and equipment that often requires professional installation. Depending on the subfloor, a vapor barrier or wood sleepers (wood members embedded in concrete that serve to support and to fasten subflooring to the floor) may be necessary. And, unless the hardwood strips are factory-finished, sanding and sealing the floor add to the expense. Engineered floors fall somewhere between these two extremes. They can cost as much as solid hardwood, but do-it-yourself homeowners can often install them.

When ascertaining the cost of any type of flooring, take into consideration the material cost, labor costs, costs of related materials, tools or equipment, and the amount of time installation will require. Make sure to ask whether any materials need to be acclimated to their site before or after installation. While this may not add to the installation cost itself, you do need to know whether you'll be able to use the new room right away, or whether the finish on your bedroom floor dictates a couple of nights at a hotel.

- If you use colors the way they appear in nature, then the darker colors should be on the lower portions of the room. Dark colors carry more visual weight.
- The best room color schemes should have a single dominant color.
- Colors appear darker and more intense in large areas than in small ones, particularly in spaces where light is reflected, strengthening the color vibrations.
- Color on aged surfaces usually displays a yellow component due to the yellowing of the finish.
- Wood and metal colors should be factored into color schemes.

Color

If you crave color underfoot, be grateful that you were born into our modern times. There are no more color taboos of taste or décor, and modern technological advances keep on producing familiar materials in unfamiliar shades and new materials in a huge array of colors. Given that anything is possible, here are a few general color rules (to be broken with good reason).

Make color part of your flooring design vocabulary. A red and white rubber floor, supremely practical, brings life to a laundry room.

Color	Effect on space	Effect on mood
Light colors, pale neutrals, bleached woods	enlarges space, makes space airy	quiet or tranquil
Medium-value nonintense colors, neutrals, fruitwood	diminishes space slightly	conservative
Deep colors, dark stained woods, black	diminishes space, erases boundaries, lowers ceilings	dramatic or traditional, old-fashioned
Autumn colors, Mahogany, rosewood	diminishes space substantially	cozy, rich, very warm
Pale blue or green	enlarges space	serene, suggests the sky
Dark blue or green	diminishes space	mysterious, suggests the sea, cool
Yellow	enlarges spaces	suggests sunshine in good lighting

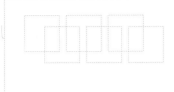

Style

What Goes with What

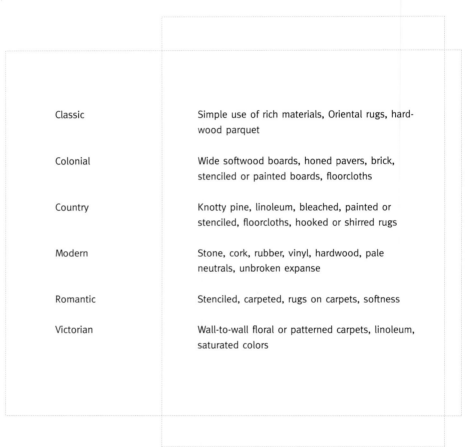

Classic	Simple use of rich materials, Oriental rugs, hardwood parquet
Colonial	Wide softwood boards, honed pavers, brick, stenciled or painted boards, floorcloths
Country	Knotty pine, linoleum, bleached, painted or stenciled, floorcloths, hooked or shirred rugs
Modern	Stone, cork, rubber, vinyl, hardwood, pale neutrals, unbroken expanse
Romantic	Stenciled, carpeted, rugs on carpets, softness
Victorian	Wall-to-wall floral or patterned carpets, linoleum, saturated colors

Classic

Colonial

Country

Modern

Romantic

Victorian

Flooring
Factors

Noise/Tactile

When it comes to the way floors sound and feel, remember that flooring materials are divided into "hard" and "soft." Soft flooring materials are the most resilient—cork, linoleum, vinyl, rubber, and carpeting. These are the quiet flooring materials: They dampen and absorb sound. Hard flooring includes ceramic tile, concrete, metal, stone, and, to a lesser degree, wood. These materials reflect sound. Generally speaking, the harder the material, the greater its sound-reflecting properties. Thus, wood flooring, which is softer than stone, ceramic tile, or concrete, is only marginally "hard." Even the hardest wood commonly used for flooring, which is maple, absorbs sound, though not as much as a resilient floor. Real wood feels softer than wood laminate flooring, which has the properties of hard flooring.

If a quiet floor is at the top of your list of design criteria, you have probably already considered carpets. But think about incorporating cork into your flooring plans. Cork's ability to deaden sound has long made it a favorite in recording studios, hospitals, concert halls, libraries, offices, and gyms. It is the flooring material you wish for your upstairs neighbors if you live in a noisy apartment building.

A floor composed of cork tiles is expensive, but beautiful and comfortable. If solid cork is beyond your reach, or if you don't care for the look, be aware that cork is at the core of some engineered flooring, lending sound-absorption to their properties.

Noise is an important flooring issue to consider. Stone floors reflect and magnify sound.

Cleaning and Maintenance

Even the lowest-maintenance flooring gets dirty. Floors are at the bottom of the room, and gravity being what it is, that means dust settles on them, things fall down onto them—and then there's the stuff on all those feet (and paws) that walk all over them! A floor that's heavily traveled will get very dirty—period. And, as your mother might have told you (had you been paying attention), if the floor looks clean, the room looks clean. Keep this in mind when making flooring choices. Regardless of how much you like the look of ceramic tile, it is not the right flooring material for you if you hate to wash floors. If you are allergic to dust, steer clear of deep-pile carpets because you will never be able to vacuum them enough to keep dust out of the fibers. There is no flooring material that is completely maintenance free, regardless of what sales people may try to tell you.

Left: Not least among flooring issues is that of cleaning. Do you like a floor that always looks immaculate? White is a good choice for this look; just remember that lots of maintenance keeps it looking fresh.

Above: A tile floor is a time-honored kitchen favorite. It requires daily sweeping to keep the tile surfaces from getting scratched.

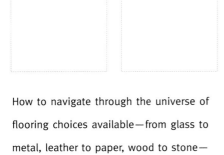

How to navigate through the universe of flooring choices available—from glass to metal, leather to paper, wood to stone— and find the one that's perfect for you.

Section 2

Flooring Solutions: New and Classic

Flooring Solutions:
New and Classic

There isn't a building material you can't put on your floor, if you have the inclination, the budget, and the right place for it. Glass? Sure—brilliantly colored glass tiles can punctuate other materials, or even shine on their own. Leather? Absolutely—this deeply natural flooring now comes in delicious designer colors. Paper? Oh, yes—it's being woven into fabulously fanciful textured rugs. Porcelain? Sure—it's very hard, and has a way with color. Metal? It's very cool—steel floors have been moving out of factories and onto the floors of the avant-garde. Plastic? Now *there's* a modern building material! It goes on and on.

Whenever a new material is invented, designers rush to find applications for it, and that includes walking on it. Of course, most flooring materials have been around for a long time, periodically rediscovered by a new generation of homeowners and decorators. That's part of the beauty of the world of flooring: It can be traditional to the point of becoming boring, until a creative designer uses a familiar material in a new way. The ways different materials are put together keep on changing, and as bonding technology gets better and better, new combinations keep popping up.

Working with Wood Laminates

The most popular floor sold in the Western world today is the wood laminate floor. No wonder: It's a brilliant use of modern materials yet traditional in its appeal to the average homeowner. Laminate flooring is versatile, affordable, can be installed by unskilled do-it-yourselfers, and it can go where wood floors can't—onto another floor, below grade, into an old house. These floors are self-contained systems that are almost unaffected by structural limitations.

Their composition comes from a chemical lab, not a forest. Layers of composite materials are compressed under high heat and sandwiched around a core that might be made of wood products or, at the product's high end, cork. Most often, the bottom consists of a paper product that acts as a vapor barrier. The floor elements come in thin (some measure as little as 1/3 inch (.84 cm) thick) tongue-and-groove planks, just like hardwood flooring, but are not nailed to the underfloor. Instead, these floors "float" on the surface. Glue holds the planks together to form a one-piece floor. At their best, wood laminate floors have a high tolerance for spills because there are no open seams where water can go. Because they are not nailed to a subfloor or to floor joists, they are not apt to develop squeaks, but they do tend to sound hollow. They do not offer the comfort of wood flooring since they are harder.

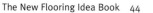

The term "wood laminate" is already a bit of a misnomer. The early wood laminates resembled hardwood, and this is still the best-selling format. Photographed wood grain finishes the top, making a high-tech product look like a traditional wood floor. But laminate floors today are made to resemble stone as well as complex wood patterns such as herringbone, parquet tile, and contrasting checkerboard weaves. Since all these designs are photographs (of parquet or of stone), there is no limit to the possible appearance of a laminate floor. The surface characteristics of the material it resembles are embossed or molded into the wear layer; ever-better photo printing technology provides the visuals, and the result is pure alchemy.

Be aware that the characteristic shine of laminate tends to be visible at the edges of recesses in the material: there are connoisseurs who claim that they can always recognize a laminate floor. But twentieth century advances in vinyls and laminates have been so progressive that generalizations are nearly impossible. Use them instead of stone, ceramic tile, cork, rubber, or linoleum if you want those looks for less. Digital technology doesn't stop with hard flooring materials. The latest carpet technology applies computer know-how by using sophisticated dye-injection processes to print digital images onto the surface of the fibers. Patterns take details from the modern world, from satellite images to interactive Web sites, as reference. This is an unapologetically high-tech floor covering for twenty-first-century homes.

Stained concrete has achieved new levels of sophistication and aesthetics. Today's staining or etching products can achieve results that combine the traditional appeal of stone with seamless modernism. The easiest to use are applied to cured concrete with sprayers such as super-sized plant misters or insect sprayers. To date, about half a dozen colors are available, with more coming onto the market all the time.

Top Left: The world of flooring no longer breaks down into "hardwood taste, soft-wood budget."

Top Middle: Metal is one of the new flooring materials currently favored by architects and designers in lofts and other modern interiors. Sensible handrails provide safety and security with these metal stairs.

Top Right: The well-loved wood laminate floor brings together the best of modern technology, traditional good looks, and ease of installation.

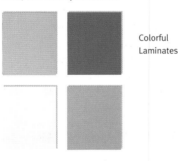

Colorful Laminates

Stained Concrete

Latex-backed Woven Paper

Left: Yesterday, wood laminate was considered the cutting edge in flooring. Today, the technology replicates other materials; in this version it could be called "stone laminate."

Right: Stained concrete is supremely modern: It can be colored and waxed to match any décor; it is tough, and an integral part of the structure.

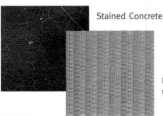

Stone

Ancient and venerable, stone is nevertheless a sophisticated modern flooring material. From a design perspective, stone is at its best after years of use, unlike other materials, which are best new. In twelfth-century European cathedrals, we walk on flagstones and stair treads that have been gently shaped by thousands of feet over hundreds of years. The stone is worn, but far from worn out. What the years of use have done is to add immeasurably to the floor's beauty. Stone is the rare thing that actually improves with age. Continued use bestows a mellow patina, so that even the simplest of stone floors eventually achieves a luxurious dignity. Stone flooring is associated with security, permanence, and solidity, and for good reason—it lasts virtually forever.

Stone is less cumbersome to install than you might think; modern cutting technology produces stone flooring tiles that measure a slender $^1/_4$ inch (.5 cm). (As with any floor, however, do confirm that the subflooring is sound.) Elaborate center medallions and decorative borders, once the exclusive purview of the wealthy, are now available as separate components in home centers and building supply stores. At the sumptuous end of the spectrum, 48-inch by 24-inch (122 cm by 61 cm) slabs can be custom-fitted to a room, resulting in a sleek floor with the unparalleled visual impact created by the stone's natural markings flowing over a large unbroken surface. Designers also achieve beautiful results with recycled old stone—roofing slates become flooring tiles; limestone flags from demolished French farmhouses see new life in American kitchens.

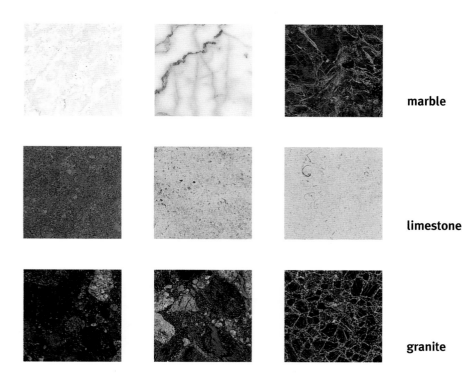

marble

limestone

granite

Known Stone

When you install stone flooring, you will want to incorporate its natural beauty into the room's overall design scheme. Stone differs from cement and tile, the other hard flooring materials, in that it is not manufactured. From a design standpoint, stone has more in common with hardwood; it is a natural product whose decorative features of color and pattern are intrinsic.

The varieties of stone most commonly used for flooring are:
- Marble
- Limestone
- Slate
- Granite

Limestone, slate, and marble in natural, honed, or aged finishes (without a high shine) are stylistically suited to rustic, Arts and Crafts (Mission), or Moderne (Mid-Century Modern) house styles.

Polished marble in colors ranging all the way from black to white is a traditional favorite in formal entries, galleries, and high-style traditional rooms. Today it is also the flooring material of choice for lavish spa baths.

The amber, cream, taupe, and gray tones of limestone, combined with its porous surface texture, make it a favorite in farmhouse kitchens. Limestone slabs with pronounced patterning are design favorites for dramatic living rooms.

Slate is extremely dense, does not burn or stain, and has a distinctive flake. Long used for hearths, it is also a bathroom favorite. Slate is newly popular in kitchens and in rooms designed to bring in the ambiance of the out-of-doors.

Because stone is so durable, it is well suited to entry halls, stairs, kitchens, bathrooms, and other high-traffic areas. The luxurious aspect of stone flooring makes it an ever more popular choice for living rooms, where area rugs are the logical choice to soften walking surfaces and dull sound. The shiniest types of stone flooring—polished marbles and granites—are also the slipperiest, so a reliable nonskid pad under rugs is important from a safety standpoint.

Stone is a cold material, a fact that once made stone floors traditional in dairies. If you are considering a stone floor, think about installing underfloor heating. Modern stone floors are easily installed over radiant electric or hot-water heating systems, and, once warm, the stone's mass holds the heat for a long time.

Stone is expensive—despite better quarrying, cutting, and installation technologies, a stone floor still costs more than its ceramic tile counterpart. However, the cost of the stone floor is quite reasonable when the price is amortized over its long life. This longevity makes stone inadvisable in stylistically dated patterns, unless the homeowner wants a time capsule underfoot.

Left: Because it is so durable, stone can be recycled and adaptively resued. This earth-toned kitchen floor was once a slate roof.

Middle: Stone floors can be highly polished and formal or rough and rustic. What they have in common is the fact that their beauty transcends the moment, getting bettter with time.

Right: Polished marble flooring is formal, dramatic, and makes a strong design statement in a small entry hall.

The characteristic good looks of dark gray or black slate are practical as well as handsome in a bathroom.

TERRAZZO PIZZAZZ

TERRAZZO IS OFTEN PRESENTED AS AN ANCIENT STONE PRODUCT AND, WHILE IT IS STONE, IT IS ACTUALLY A TWENTIETH-CENTURY BUILDING MATERIAL DESCENDED FROM THE ART OF MOSAIC AND ORIGINALLY KNOWN AS CONCRETE MOSAIC. MARBLE CHIPS MIXED WITH COLORED PORTLAND CEMENT FORM A MATRIX THAT IS POURED OVER A CONCRETE BASE AND STABILIZED BY MEANS OF METAL DIVIDER STRIPS. ONCE CURED, IT IS GROUND AND POLISHED TO A SMOOTH FINISH OR, LESS OFTEN, LEFT IN A RUSTICATED STATE.

TODAY'S TERRAZZO IS THINNER, MAKING IT MORE USEFUL FOR HOMES. BEAUTIFUL AND STRONG, THIS IS A GOOD CHOICE FOR THOSE WHO WANT STONE FLOORING WITH A MORE TECHNOLOGICAL LOOK OR A PATTERN COMPLEXITY THAT'S EITHER UNAVAILABLE OR PROHIBITIVELY COSTLY IN SOLID STONE. BECAUSE OF ITS METHOD OF CONSTRUCTION, TERRAZZO IS WELL SUITED TO THE SMOOTH, CURVY DESIGNS OF THE ART DECO AND MODERNE STYLES, WHICH ARE CURRENTLY SEEING A STRONG REVIVAL IN INTERIOR-DESIGN SCHEMES.

SOME OF THE MOST INTERESTING TERRAZZO FLOORS USE THE METAL DIVIDER STRIPS AS PART OF THE DESIGN STATEMENT. MOST OFTEN BRASS, THEY CAN BE COPPER, NICKEL, SILVER, ZINC, STEEL, OR ANY OTHER METAL WHOSE COLORS FORM A THIN CONTRASTING OR COMPLEMENTARY BORDER BETWEEN FIELD COLORS. THE MATERIAL IS NOT LIMITED TO MARBLE MIXTURES, EITHER. ONYX, TRAVERTINE, SERPENTINE, EVEN GLASS, CAN CREATE TERRAZZO PIZZAZZ.

Terrazzo is not new technology, but in homes it always looks fresh and surprising.

Flooring Solutions:
Wood

Wood—Classic and Cutting Edge

Few materials can withstand the test of time quite the way that wood does. A natural wood floor gives a room unmistakable warmth, reflects natural light, and fits in seamlessly with almost any décor. And a good-quality wood floor can last a century or more—just take a look at some of the beautiful, turn-of-the-century wood floors in landmark homes today.

But choosing a wood floor is not as simple as calling a contractor and ordering one. You have to consider the type of wood, the application, and the color and finish—and each decision you make will affect the overall look of the room. Solid wood floors do have some limitations. They are not the best choice for areas that tend to get wet because wood expands and contracts when exposed to dampness. Installation itself poses some problems, too. Most wood floors must be nailed into place, making them poor choices for basements and other rooms constructed on concrete slabs. And newly installed wood floors might come up as much as 3/4 inch (2 cm) from where the previous floor was, creating a troublesome and potentially hazardous little step up from one room to another. ■ ■ ■

Luckily, modern manufacturers have offered solutions that make wood floors more accessible. Floating laminate floors in simulated wood grain can be installed in basements and kitchen without worry and can float easily over concrete subfloors.

Wood is for warmth: its hues, texture, and sound quality play to the senses.

Engineered wood flooring combines the best of wood and high-tech materials. A distant descendant of plywood, an engineered wood plank has a top wear layer of solid wood applied to alternating layers of other wood materials. Because the layers are perpendicular to each other, there is great strength in this type of wood flooring. An advantage of engineered wood flooring is the fact that, unlike solid wood, it can be installed as "floating flooring."

Finger joining offers another alternative to the way hardwood has traditionally been sold: in strips 2 $1/4$" (7 cm) wide and $3/4$" (2 cm) thick. Finger-joined boards are composed of small end-matched pieces bonded together, resulting in wide 7-foot (2.1 m) pieces. Environmentalists like finger-joined hardwood flooring because the smaller pieces of wood are a more efficient use of natural resources. And, the uniform lengths result in shorter installation times and thus, lower overall cost.

Factory-applied finishes are a great boon to homeowners; as soon as the wood floor has been installed, it can be used. Factory finishes are uniform and applied under dust-free, temperature-controlled conditions for optimal curing. Polyurethane, when exposed to ultraviolet light, cures almost instantly. Now urethane factory finishes are routinely uv-light cured. Even newer is the use of ceramic or aluminum oxides in the finish. Although the amounts are too small and the particles too fine to be visible, ceramic or aluminum oxides mixed with polyurethane make for an extremely tough surface layer.

If you simply must have real wood, consider parquet flooring—made of smaller pieces of wood glued into tiles that can be glued into place—which can add real-wood character to rooms where nails won't work.

If you're looking for something as beautiful as wood and as tough as stone, acrylic-impregnated wood flooring—natural wood pressure treated with a tough-as-nails acrylic finish that goes right through the entire plank—is yet another option. With the color and finish penetrating every pore of the wood, these floors are highly resistant to scratches, scuffs, and moisture, and so can boldly go where few wood floors have gone before—the mudroom, entryway, kitchen, and beyond. Available in the same styles as wood laminate, acrylic-impregnated floors are often used in commercial spaces where foot traffic (including wet, muddy feet) is high and have recently become available to residential customers as well.

Style, Substance, and Pattern

Once you've decided on wood, you need to think about the style and substance of your floor. Think not only about the wood itself but also the installation. For example, if your room is long and somewhat narrow, a straight installation of thin hardwood planks will be your best bet—the repeated lines make the room look wider. You can add a high-gloss finish that reflects natural light to further the illusion of space. Even the sound quality of the wood floor, a warm yet definite echo, suggests a room of larger dimensions.

Planked horizontal installations of wood can make long narrow rooms look subtly wider.

A Palette in Wood

Oak with oil finish

Red Oak

Unstained Oak

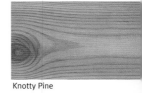

Planked Birch

Mahogany

Knotty Pine

Cardamom Stain

Saffron Stain

Cobalt Stain

A large, open room makes an ideal setting for experimenting with pattern. A herringbone pattern creates interest on the floor while at the same time making the room appear less vacuous. And a room that is defined by architectural details—a stunning hearth, built-in bookcases, or floor-to-ceiling French doors—benefits from inlaid borders that draw the eye out toward the perimeter of the room.

Put similar thought into your choice of wood. A high-traffic kitchen might demand a tough hardwood like oak or maple, while less-traveled bedrooms could work just as well with soft, warm knotty pine. Think about the grain and overall look of the wood, and consider how it fits in with your personal style. Are you going for a modern, streamlined look? The heavy grain of oak or walnut might not work as well in your ultra-modern loft space, but thin planks of clear beech might be just your style.

And what about color? Once installed, a floor can be finished in an endless variety of tones—ash, for example, while beautiful in its natural state, takes on an entirely different character when stained a deep cherry, and achieves another look altogether when tinted colonial blue.

Matching your floor to your furnishing is important, but perhaps less important than one might think. While the style of the floor should complement the décor and dimensions of the room, matching the floor precisely to the furnishings might be a mistake. For example, gorgeous Georgian furniture of deep, dark cherry is lost when matched with a floor of the same wood, stain, and finish. But a floor of bright, unstained natural oak or maple, with a semi gloss finish and trimmed out with matching floor molding, creates a stunning but subtle backdrop, while the furniture plays a starring role.

Wood floors also offer flexibility. They make beautiful backdrops for antique or unique area rugs, which can be used to warm up rooms during cold winter months, and removed to reveal a cooler-looking and airier space in the heat of summer. This option allows a homeowner to dramatically change the look and feel of a room without making major renovations.

Tile

When you install a tile floor, you have the opportunity to create something personal and unique while following in the footsteps of countless generations of homeowners before you. The Egyptians invented fired-clay tile six thousand years ago; successive civilizations have never tired of reinventing the basic formula. Universal and familiar, the humble clay tile is often taken for granted, yet it is so versatile that its design possibilities are virtually limitless. And, in recent years, tiles have gone high-tech. Now there are aluminum tiles with a baked-enamel finish, steel tiles, cement tiles with a terra-cotta surface, glass tiles, and plastic tiles.

Whatever their makeup, all tiles are really just thin surfacing units that can be used individually or as part of a whole. This gives them huge design potential, a fact that has always made tiles irresistible to artists. If you want a truly creative floor, whether of your own or someone else's design, tiles can provide it.

Designing with tile can broadcast a message with wit, style, and subtlety. Use tiles to express something ethnic, geographic, historic, or personal about you or your house. Make a sophisticated statement with a high-tech combination of glass and metal, or plastic and baked earth. Celebrate colors in your natural environment. You'll find countless choices represented in the variety offered for sale, which may be the downside of shopping for flooring tiles. The world of tiles is vast and seductive; you can easily get lost in the grout. A tile floor, perhaps more than any other kind, calls for forethought. That involves commonsense basics, such as measuring and drawing out a floor plan of the room to scale. But think as well about color, tone, mood, scale, complexity of pattern, and range of colors. A striking design can become meaningless in a flooring footprint interspersed with furniture, wall cutouts, bays, and islands. Too-small or predictable patterns can look timid and frumpy. Borders can make a room look cluttered if not designed to echo the architecture, or at least fool us into thinking that it does. Colors that are scrumptious in 12-inch (30 cm) swatches can become a problem in an overall design. ■ ■ ■

At the same time, tile is a supremely practical flooring material with a long history in kitchens, bathrooms, entry halls, and other hard-wearing places that tend to get wet. The price range is nearly as vast as the selection, and tile floors can be laid by do-it-yourselfers (though elaborate installations are best done by those with some experience). One of the easiest kinds of tile to install is called ceramic mosaic. Smaller than than common tile, it is manufactured in sheets held together by a mesh backing. The backing offers correct spacing for the grout, which is applied later.

Ceramic tile, more than any other flooring material, is associated with colorful, ethnic design statements.

Tile flooring is one of the best ways to create a rustic design scheme full of irregular, patinated surfaces and earth tones. The familiar quarry tile is an ever-popular choice. Until recently it was only available in terra-cotta red, but now runs the gamut of earth tones from the palest sand to the darkest umber. Tiles are just as helpful for those drawn to the other end of the style spectrum—one route to a clean, hard-edged design is to lay a floor of precisely cut, smooth ceramic tile. Tile is created equally in the artisan's shop and in the automated factory; the smooth, mass-produced product is not considered better than the earthy handmade one. Each is perfectly suited to its intended use.

Guide to Glaze

Glazed tiles are made in various sizes and shapes and most lend themselves to floors. But high-gloss tiles should be used cautiously, both because of the danger of slipping and because a mirror glaze is easily scratched by grit carried into houses on shoes. One glaze that's been developed for tiles is known as a crystal glaze; it has a rough, granular texture, which is more or less slip-proof. Crystal-glazed tiles are among the most popular for floors.

Unglazed ceramic tile is a strong favorite for contemporary flooring. Part of its appeal is its association with warmth. Much beautiful unglazed floor tile comes from Mexico, and few things hold heat better than dark-colored, unglazed quarry tiles (hence their long history in solariums and greenhouses). But they are creeping into the rest of the house, especially in the desert Southwest, Florida, and California. From a design standpoint, unglazed quarry tiles or pavers can be used in any room of the house, except for the most formally decorated ones.

Tile's other design personality is sleek, modern, and monochromatic. Tiles are supremely versatile, both in materials and manufacturing processes and in their uses.

A Palette in Tile

Unglazed Stone Tile

Metallic Glazed

Wheel Thrown Tile

Crackle Glaze Tile

Glazed Clay Tile

Handpainted Tile

Iridescent Glass Tile

Terra-cotta Tile

Floral Tile

About Grout

Grout, the material that fills the joints between tiles, can make the floor more interesting. For graphic impact, chose a grout color that contrasts sharply with the tile. For a monochromatic, quiet effect, chose grout the same color as the tile. The grout is, in fact, an integral element when considering a tile floor, not as glamorous, but important to the design, expense, ease of maintenance, and long-term wear.

Also, tile is unforgiving of uneven subfloors. Specialists say that a 4-inch (10 cm) layer of perfectly smooth, level material must support a tile floor. If your floor flexes or has hills and valleys, then this is not the flooring for you.

Cork and Rubber

Fifty years after enjoying status as the flooring material of choice for style-conscious home-owners, cork is back. Actually, it is more accurate to say that the same cork that was such an important element in mid-century modern design is still very much in use. What is more, it was in use long before minimalist designers discovered its superb qualities as a building material. Cork was among the earliest resilient flooring products, and it has never complete-ly gone out of style.

It's no wonder. Cork has resilience, natural good looks, and superb sound-deadening prop-erties. It appeals to environmentalists because harvesting cork does not kill the cork oak tree. Grown primarily in Portugal and Spain, these trees can be stripped of their outer layer peri-odically, with no detrimental effect on the tree itself. A single tree yields cork over the span of 100 to 150 years.

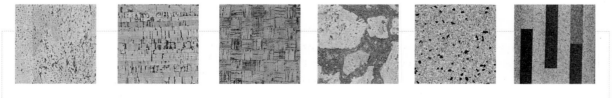

Decorative Veneer Cork

A Palette in Cork

Scuff-proof

All varieties of resilient flooring, including cork and rubber, have a convenient ability to bounce back from scuffs and abrasions. Resilience, which also makes for comfort underfoot, comes in thin sheets and tiles. That means imperfections in your subflooring will show through, and may eventually lead to wear and deterioration. The importance of a good subfloor can't be overstated. It must be smooth, dry, and flat, and it must be free of dirt, grease, paint, or anything else that would hinder a good bond with the floor tiles' backing.

Marbled rubber floor tile is making a style comeback after years of absence. Its wonderful look is matched with toughness. Floors such as these are good for fifty years or more.

Carpet and Rugs

For homeowners craving a new look, a spot of color, a pattern to unify a room, or simply some fun and excitement in the décor, change is as close as a new rug. Imagine, for instance, the joy of a giant flower on your floor, its shape delineated by its great, curving, purple petals. New carpets aren't limited to squares, rectangles, circles, or ovals; their shapes can be very free-form indeed.

As for carpet color and design, the two newest trends aim for polar opposite effects. One applies pattern and color in the most high-tech way possible. Digital images are printed onto carpets via computerized dye-injection processes. Though any type of pattern is possible, early examples have featured images that draw on technology for inspiration, including satellite images and Web site graphics.

The other trend uses a modern dyeing process called tea staining to make brand new carpets look old. The term is a misnomer; no Earl Gray is actually used. For the gently aged look of an antique Oriental, modern dyes produce an overall amber cast that speak of elegant age but do not damage the carpet fibers in the process. Early efforts at weaving these shadings into the carpet proved unconvincing; tea staining is more successful at achieving this beloved look. ■■■

Beyond Traditional Wool

The best carpets are made of wool, woven either on a wool or cotton base, and the best carpet wool comes from New Zealand. Wool is strong, soft, and superbly dyeable. It is, however, expensive. Alternative fibers have been used since they were invented; some will provide the look for less but will not give the same consistent quality of wear. Recent favorites include sisal, coir, and seagrass. Seagrass is lovely, pale, and somewhat fragile, with the bonus of a faint but characteristic scent. Coir and, to a lesser degree, sisal, have a coarser texture than wool. Both have natural good looks in brown tones. Coir, especially, will rot if it gets wet; use coir carpeting only in areas not exposed to possible moisture.

The same is true of the new paper rugs, which make sly allusions to the look of wicker or the deep-shag carpeting fad of the 1950s. Their best use is in bedrooms, conversation corners, or other low-traffic areas.

Much modern carpeting can be custom-pieced for individual designs. You might, for instance, have stair carpeting climb up and down the steps in a color progression. Or you might choose contrasting or complementary colors for a carpet's body and border.

New paper-based materials let carpets mimic woven rush and tatami textures.

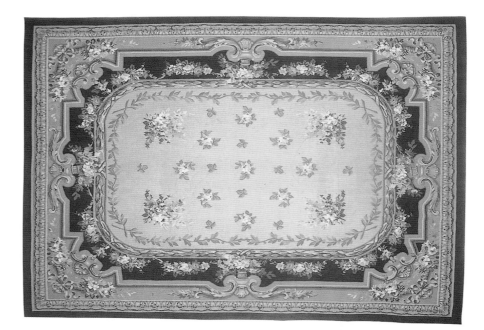

Enjoy the shaded tones of elegant antiquity in a new rug.

Floor Art for Sale

Carpets and rugs are brilliant examples of home furnishings as art. Utilitarian floor coverings are exemplars of local craft traditions all over the world. We take our carpets to heart in ways usually expressed among other flooring choices only by purists. People who love carpets love them a lot, and we see that reflected in everything associated with the world of rugs and carpeting. As with all forms of art, record prices are paid and misinformation abounds, so education pays off.

You can buy a piece of art for your floor without fear if you follow these guidelines:

- Buy from reputable dealers. An Oriental rug sold for an alleged 80 percent off during an oft-repeated going-out-of-business sale is likely not to be the rare beauty it's represented to be. Oriental carpet dealers with stable, customer-based businesses, on the other hand, can be vast and personable fonts of information on the subject. Many are delighted to educate potential customers and will happily answer questions. A reputable dealer will always tell you where your rug is from, what it is made of (wool, cotton, silk, and whether the dyes are vegetable or aniline), how it is made, and will let you take it home to try it out. Antiques dealers should be willing to take back a carpet and refund your money for any reason.

- Don't shop for art if what you really want is a red rug. There is such a wealth of choice available in the commercial carpet world that you may want to stop and consider whether you really want an antique hooked rug or the warm and colorful statement it makes. The antique is fragile and costly, and the current wave of appreciation for this appealing folk art form has spawned many companies that make new, practical versions.

- Please yourself. The best reason to put a piece of flooring art into your home is because you love it. With all the options that are out there, don't let yourself be pressured into buying what's chic, what's a good investment, what the most fashionable people you know say you should. You'll be looking at that carpet for a long time; make sure it will continue to bring you pleasure. That way, you'll still be happy even if the bottom drops out of the market for it, or if tastemakers change their minds about the design.

A Palette
in Carpet

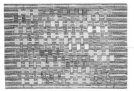

Flat Weave

Aubusson

Kilim

Needlepoint

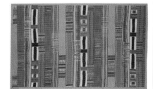

Dashiki Pattern

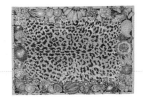

Needlepoint

START WITH THE CARPET

A TRADITIONAL PIECE OF INTERIOR DESIGN WISDOM HOLDS THAT, FOR A ROOM'S COLOR SCHEME, YOU SHOULD TAKE YOUR CUES FROM YOUR CARPET. LIKE MANY OLD SAWS THAT HAVE BEEN REPEATED INTO MEANINGLESSNESS, IT STILL HOLDS A KERNEL OF TRUTH.

CHOOSE TWO OR, AT MOST, THREE COLORS FROM A ROOM-SIZED ORIENTAL RUG FOR THE ROOM'S FABRICS AND WALLS. HARMONY WILL RESULT, AND IT IS INFINITELY EASIER THAN IT IS TO TRY TO MATCH A CARPET TO ALREADY-EXIST-ING FURNITURE AND TEXTILES.

Glass and Porcelain

Of all the materials you might think to use to cover your floor, one of the more surprising, surely, is glass. To some of us it seems antithetical to walk on a substance so prone to shattering, one we associate with transparency, mirrors, and windows.

Great Looks in Glass

Yet glass is an extremely strong material that, when poured in thickness beyond what's required for windows, is nearly indestructible. Glass has an unsurpassed way with color, hardness that makes it a snap to keep clean, and comes in flooring formats that offer great value and design versatility. Glass flooring is impervious to frost, water, and stains, and highly resistant to chemical attack, fading, or discoloration.

A glass floor can be the ultimate statement about texture or color. It can be graphic, from modern to deco, or it can be sleek, neutral, and understated. It is always stunning. Remember that the single best feature of glass as a design tool is its ability to reflect, deepen, and echo color. Some glass tiles are fused, some poured into molds, and in some, the colors are painted onto the back. Each technique creates a different effect. An especially well-loved glass tile features the gentle, time-dulled surface of beach glass. The colors are powdery and soft but saturated as only glass colors can be.

As lavish and delicate as they look, these beautiful floors are cleaned with nothing more than a swipe of common glass cleaner. They should never be waxed but can be damp-mopped just like a tile floor.

THE LEADING CHARACTERISTIC OF GLASS AND PORCELAIN—HARDNESS—ALSO PRESENTS A SAFETY HAZARD. UNLESS YOUR GLASS OR PORCELAIN FLOOR IS MADE WITH A TEXTURED SURFACE, SMOOTHNESS IS APT TO BECOME SLICK WHEN WET. INSTALL WITH SAFETY IN MIND: PUT FLOOR-GRIPPING RUBBERIZED MATS ON A BATHROOM FLOOR, KEEP GLITTERING INSTALLATIONS OUT OF THE PATH OF FAST-MOVING CHILDREN AND OF ADULTS UNSURE OF THEIR FOOTING. NEVER PUT A SCATTER RUG OVER GLASS OR PORCELAIN TILES WITHOUT AN UNDERLAY DESIGNED TO STOP SKIDDING. DON'T USE GLASS OR PORCELAIN FOR STAIR TREADS.

The clear colors of glass and porcelain are heightened by water and work well in bathrooms.

While you may not be ready for a roomful of glass underfoot, consider the design possibilities of setting glass tile into other materials. Here is an opportunity to add dimension to any floor; you might incorporate a subtly reflective border, pick out one color to accentuate or lend cohesion, or carry some design element into the floor in unexpected ways. Imagine the surprise of a thin line of cobalt blue or ruby red glittering in the quiet of an oak floor, or of an iridescent highlight in a floor of unglazed quarry tile.

One of the most exciting options available in flooring today is a glass mosaic rug resembling a classic Oriental or kilim. Small pieces of glass in all colors of the rainbow, from soft iridescent pastels to bold jewel tones, make up the carpet pattern, which can be set into nearly any kind of flooring. Designs are made to order and shipped on fiberglass mesh for easy installation with thin-set mortar and grout.

Porcelain Possibilities

In hardness, porcelain lies somewhere between glass and glazed ceramic. It is made from a white, nonporous clay that, when fired, has all the characteristics desired in fine tableware. Porcelain floor tiles are extremely hard and can be easily cleaned with glass cleaner, something that's not recommended for clay. Porcelain floor tiles do not provide the same richness and depth of color as glass but have equal resistance to staining, etching, and temperature fluctuations. They can be as versatile as clay tiles. Some porcelain floor tiles are as smooth as a dinner plate, while others resemble limestone.

Clear glass field tiles alternate with jewel-toned smaller tiles in a design whose brilliance belies its toughness.

A Palette
in Glass

Clear Glass Tile

Colored Glass Tile

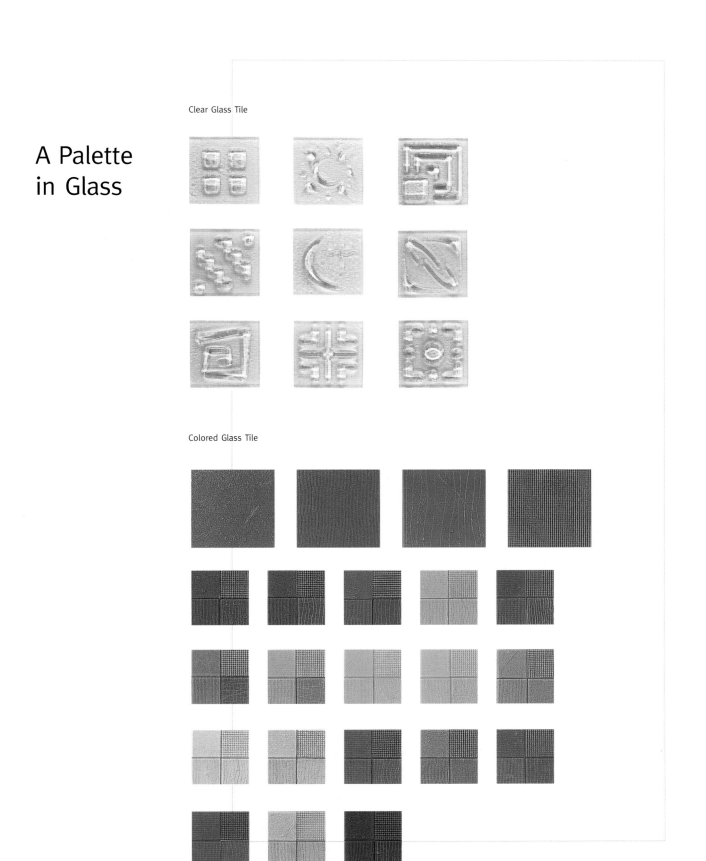

With a beautiful floor as a base, even a sparsely appointed room can look elegant and rich. Ordinary furniture takes on dignity, an almost-empty room can look glamorous and mysterious.

Section 3
Designing with Flooring

Designing
with Flooring

Think of installing a new floor as a design opportunity; uninspired architecture can be lifted beyond the banal, less-than-pleasing proportions can be corrected. Because flooring has the ability to either fade into the background or dominate the room, its design potential is vast.

Use saturated color on the floor to bring a room's shape into focus or to correct the well-like claustrophobia of overly high ceilings in a small room. For an interesting jewel-box effect, try tinting the ceiling in a lighter version of the same color. A border can correct, or appear to correct, the shape of an awkward room; stencil, tile, paint, or use carpeting or resilient flooring to outline the shape of the room as you prefer to see it.

Especially if the design of a room or house is not to your liking, use flooring to create walking and seating areas. In an open layout, bold contrast leads the eye away from the parts you want to de-emphasize. If a house is chopped up into small rooms with little cohesion, use an overall pattern on the whole floor to unify space.

Instead of placing a carpet under the dining room table, where it will require constant cleaning and pose a possible safety hazard, define a rectangle around the table and chairs in a band of contrasting flooring. The greatest drama is achieved with a material different from that of the rest of the floor: wood timbers laid into stone, tiles set into wood, glass tiles into terra-cotta pavers. For a subtle and sophisticated effect, use different materials in similar colors.

To set off a kitchen cooking area or preparation island, outline it in flooring different from the rest of the room. ■ ■ ■

A small room can be made to look larger with a floor that's lighter than the walls. Keep in mind that every line of contrast constricts space; a pale expanse looks larger than one broken up with pattern.

If you want to bring the outdoors into a room, choose flooring that harmonizes with an element of nature seen from a window or door. This could include wood flooring in a species of tree growing outside, stone that echoes colors in the environment, or colors like that of a distant body of water. The most natural effects are achieved with materials that are not polished to a high sheen.

To play up the organic charm of an informal country kitchen, scatter small tiles in an irregular, seemingly random pattern onto a floor tiled with larger pavers. Do not space them too closely; if the room is large, use two different sizes of small tiles.

Large, alternating squares, whether in stone, resilient materials, or painted, give cohesion and a sense of design purpose to an irregularly shaped room. On the other hand, this traditional flooring approach can make a rectangular room look boxy.

Installed in a border long enough to repeat the pattern again and again, mosaic border designs can achieve a sense of movement and rhythm.

Top Left: Material and elevation can give a floor lots of impact; this light-filled sitting area becomes a special retreat, set off from the rest of the room.

Top Right: The colors and the rustic beauty of nature continue into an entrance hall paved with slate.

Bottom Right: Pattern, color, atmosphere, architecture—all can be created, altered, or emphasized by stenciling the floor. What's more, this is one craft that does not call for artistic expertise, just attention to detail.

Hardwood
and Softwood

Because it's been a favorite flooring material for so very long, wood's design potential has been explored in every imaginable way. Or so it seems, until contemporary flooring companies begin to produce wood flooring in new colors or combined with other materials in new ways or to bring a new wood variety into the mix. Sometimes they even (gasp!) use hardwoods and softwoods together. ■ ■ ■

Hardwoods versus Soft

The difference between hardwood and softwood is, obviously, one of degrees of hardness. In flooring, this translates into qualities of wear and cost. Hardwoods tend to be longer lasting, less vulnerable to scratches and nicks, and more expensive than softwood. But there is a place for softwood flooring in the modern home. Some of the softer woods, notably the pines, firs, and larches, are loved for their distinctive patterns and colors. Generally, softwood floorboards are available in wider widths than hardwoods. The look of a pine floor is a style icon: If you want this in your country kitchen, you have a practical option in extremely hard factory-applied finishes that incorporate suspended metal particles and are cured with ultraviolet light.

Wood floor strips and planks are usually laid perpendicular to the floor joists, but if the subfloor is sound, wood flooring can be laid diagonally. Another way of achieving design interest is with a herringbone pattern of narrow strips. Both the diagonal and the herringbone patterns can be useful in correcting unfortunate proportions. A too-narrow hall, for instance, can appear wider with a herringbone-patterned floor.

Some of the specialty finishes include bleaching, pickling, antiquing, and coloring. Strong caution is advised to do-it-yourselfers, however; these are best applied at the factory, since they can damage the wood and can cause personal injury and environmental damage.

A RADIANT FLOOR

The news about under-floor radiant heat is that it can now be installed under wood floors. Today's flooring professionals cite advances in manufacturing, such as finger-joining, which has recently brought this economical and practical heating technology to wood for utterly comfortable flooring. The systems are best suited to narrow-strip hardwood floors that experience minimal seasonal expansion and contraction; planks over 3 inches (8 cm) wide won't work. A network of hot-water-filled tubing runs under the floor, warming it and the room. The water in the system is continuously returned to the water heater for constant, even heat.

A QUICK GLOSSARY OF STAINS AND FINISHES

SPECIALTY FINISHES AND STAINS ARE WAYS TO EXPAND YOUR DESIGN OPTIONS WITH WOOD FLOORS. HERE'S A QUICK RUNDOWN:

STAINS DARKEN THE WOOD BUT PRESERVE THE APPEARANCE OF THE GRAIN. CLEAR FINISHES SHOWCASE THE NATURAL COLOR AND GRAIN. VARNISHES AND SHELLACS PROVIDE A HARD FINISH BUT ARE NOT WATERPROOF, WHILE URETHANES ARE. LACQUERS ARE MORE WATER-RESISTANT THAN VARNISHES AND SHELLACS BUT ARE SUSCEPTIBLE TO CRACKING AND PEELING. ACID-CURING SWEDISH FINISHES ARE FAST-DRYING AND RESIST YELLOWING. PENETRATING FINISHES PRESERVE THE APPEARANCE OF THE GRAIN WHILE SOAKING INTO WOOD PORES. THEY ARE AN EFFECTIVE WAY TO COLOR A WOOD'S NATURAL GRAIN BUT, UNLIKE STAINS, THEY LEAVE A VERY THIN FILM AT THE SURFACE.

Top Left: Wide-plank softwood flooring in an elegant setting exudes warmth and timeless style. These floorboards are old-growth larch.

Top Right: Hardwood strips can be laid in a variety of directions and patterns for design interest.

Bottom Left: The iconic country kitchen has old, old pine flooring.

Bottom Right: The finish is an integral part of wood flooring's appearance. Here, softwood planks are protected with one of the new satin finishes now available in polyurethanes.

Hardwoods

Hardwood and Softwood

Softwoods

Above: from left to right, top to bottom: White Ash, American Birch, Chestnut, Elm, Gum, Hackberry, Pecan Hickory, Magnolia, Hard Maple, Black Walnut, and Yellow Poplar.

Right: from left to right, top to bottom: Baldcypress, Eastern White Pine, Southern Pine, and Heart Pine.

Parquet
and Inlay

The newest embellishments to wood floors aren't part of the wood itself but, rather, decorative images composed of aluminum oxide particles embedded into many layers of polyurethane. In other words, the embellishment is part of the finish. Patterns and colors usually only found in painted and stenciled floors come ready-made as tongue-and-groove planks in standard widths, ready to pop into an otherwise sober wood floor.

Parquet and inlay used to be the most deluxe of wood flooring. Now, laser technology is doing for inlay what designs embedded in the finish are doing to border stencils—providing more options at price points unheard of a short time ago.

The Latest Options

Many decorative wood inlays are still being made by highly skilled craftsmen, but the new laser-cutting techniques are reviving this classic design tradition. Individual components of the design can be constructed out of a variety of woods for three-dimensional effect. The parts are cut from 5/16-inch (.8 cm) hardwood and then joined with glue or urethane adhesive. When the inlay is dry, its edges are routed to match the tongue-and-groove joints of the rest of the floor, and the inlay is set in place. Additional drama can be created by dyeing components with aniline dyes; the color and contrast remains even after sanding.

Stock inlays are becoming plentiful, but laser-cutting technology also makes it easier to create custom designs. If you have a family crest, signature emblem, or classic favorite, it can be a rich part of the foyer floor. Some of the most popular stock designs available include center medallions and compass roses, southwestern patterns, floral and geometric borders, and a whole menagerie of animals. Any of them make fitting embellishments to the living or dining room floor, but consider how striking an oval decorative medallion might be on a stair landing. Or use a motif at the entrance to a room that signals its use.

Inlay can be used to guide the eye along a hallway or to create flow in an overall layout. Borders are popular ways of defining or stressing the definition of a room's footprint. When the border is inlaid in a different variety of wood, the effect tends to be richer and more architectural. Secondary wood varieties in the room can be beautifully echoed this way.

In both inlaid wood and finish-coat decorations, colorful designs featuring fruit and flowers are best suited to farmhouse and country interiors, while classic designs such as the Greek key can generally work in most decorative schemes. Be careful when using center medallions or other large designs. These work best in large rooms with more or less square outlines, but can easily overwhelm a small room or render an asymmetric one lopsided. Also be careful to avoid the room-shrinking effect of a border placed too far in from the walls. (Too close to the walls, on the other hand, makes it look stingy.) Before installing any kind of wood floor decoration, make a scale drawing with the decorative element also drawn to scale.

Left: Because technology has streamlined the manufacturing process, the designer-look of an imposing center medallion in the entry is now within the reach of most homeowners.

Right: Lavish border and center embellishments are now available as component parts that can be inserted into any floor.

Inlay Options

Ornate Medallion Inlay

Classic Medallion Inlay   Inlay Borders

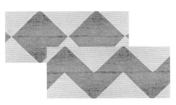

Fruit, Diamond, and Grecian Key Inlays   Diamond-pattern Plank Inlay

Parquet Options

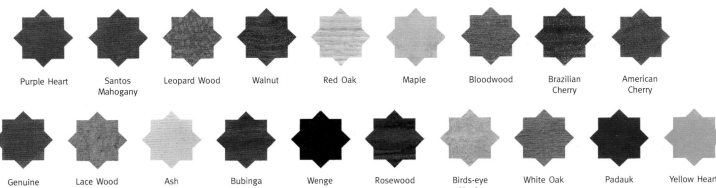

| Purple Heart | Santos Mahogany | Leopard Wood | Walnut | Red Oak | Maple | Bloodwood | Brazilian Cherry | American Cherry |

| Genuine Mahogany | Lace Wood | Ash | Bubinga | Wenge | Rosewood | Birds-eye Maple | White Oak | Padauk | Yellow Heart |

Paint
and Stencil

Lovers of wood flooring like to point out that there is no flooring type that is easier to transform completely, without the inconvenience of new construction and for minimal cost, than a wood floor. Paint can give new life to an old, worn floor or it can turn a raw new floor into a gently patinated one with the feel of an antique. You can apply an overall coat of literally any color paint for a quick fix for worn or discolored floors, and this is an economical way to finish new pine boards. Painting a floor provides an ideal opportunity to brighten or mute the room, bring a color scheme into focus, or to experiment with new color combinations.

With the right primer, old paint or finishes can usually be covered. However, flaking, chipping, or loose surface treatments should be sanded first. Many people like to use deck or boat paint on a floor, but you can use regular enamel or eggshell paints. Floors are best primed with acrylic paints that will flex with movement. After painting, the surface of the floor will be finished off with several coats of polyurethane, and you will probably want to refresh the polyurethane annually to protect the painted finish.

If you prefer a pattern to an overall coat, the tried-and-true geometric floor is an excellent design solution for a great variety of house styles, from Colonial antique to Country to Contemporary. It is achieved by careful measuring, taping, and then painting sections of the floor. The paint can be used to emulate stone, metal, leather, or any other material; a favored approach is to paint dramatically veined faux marble in contrasting light and dark colors. Or the floor can be a merry checkerboard of two favorite colors.

Another popular decorative approach to wood flooring is to stencil a pattern onto the overall floor or onto a specific area. Stenciled floors are most effective when designed to work with the room's architecture; you might want to echo or magnify a decorative element, to point out something about the style of the house, or to accentuate or minimize a floor plan. Many companies offer design, color, and technical advice, as well as ready-cut stencils. This is an indication of the fact that floor stenciling, when done with care, is a craft that even the inexperienced can carry out to great effect. ■ ■ ■

How to Stencil a Border on a Floor

Step 1: To square off a floor for stenciling, take the measurements of the floor and use them to draw a plan to scale on graph paper. Measure your stencil block and decide on an appropriate scale.

Step 2: Find and mark with chalk the centers of the walls and mark off the positions of the stencil pattern blocks, allowing for whatever space you choose between the wall and the stencil border.

Step 3: If one corner is cut off (with boxed-in pipes, for example), cut off the corner of the stenciled border and repeat this device for decorative consistency in each of the other three corners.

Step 4: If you want to add any stencils in the center of the floor, stretch a piece of heavily chalked string between the centers of both pairs of opposite walls. Where the two lines cross will be the center of the room. Working from the center, position any additional stencils at equal distances away from it.

Top Left: There is no more effective or economical way to completely change the look of a room than with a coat of paint. Here, the floor is wood, but other flooring can be painted as well.

Top Right: Even the simplest pattern stenciled onto a floor can become the basis for a decorative scheme for the entire room.

Mix and match colors to create stunning borders.

Floorcloths

Floorcloths are canvas "rugs" painted in imitation of fine flooring or carpeting as colorful and inexpensive alternatives. That is to say, they were. Today, floorcloths are highly desirable flooring in themselves, no longer considered second best. They are used like any area rug: in the hallway, in kitchens, in front of the fire. However, because floorcloths are painted canvas, they are not as durable as rugs or carpets, and they cannot be washed. Floorcloths aren't so fragile as to be impractical, however. You can walk on them, and usually a regular sweeping keeps them clean.

Floorcloths can look good in any décor, since there are no limits to their design inspiration. They are, however, a wonderfully authentic element in a country home, and many of the floorcloths offered for sale are decorated with country motifs.

Top: There are no limits to design inspiration, including that of floorcloths. For starters, they don't have to be rectangular.

Left: There are no rules that say floorcloths have to be styled in country motifs.

Above: When making your own floorcloth, draw on your own life for ideas.

Mosaics

Mosaic is the name we give to the pictures or decorative designs that are made when small pieces of colored glass, stone, or tile are set into mortar. It's an ancient craft that's always being rediscovered. In its constant re-emergence as a decorative art, mosaic is like paint on a wall—familiar, even commonplace, until the materials enter the hands of a skilled artisan. Then, the artistic expression is as fresh and new as the imagination creating it.

The pieces of stone that make up mosaic flooring are quite small, so that mosaic really is a kind of painting with stone, and mosaic floors transcend the design limitations of the medium. Mosaics are essentially made the same way now as they were when they were the chic flooring material of choice in Pompeii. Small stone pieces are selected and set into mortar by hand. This surpassingly simple technique has design flexibility that constantly puts mosaic flooring at the cutting edge of interior fashion. It's no wonder that mosaics have always stood for status flooring—they can be created in any range of colors and patterns, and from ancient civilizations on, have been used to advertise the homeowner's power—or latest enthusiasm. It's no different today. Custom mosaic flooring is limitless in color and design; this is one way of getting exactly the floor you want.

Ready-Made Mosaics

Less costly is the option of inserting ready-made mosaics into floors to create borders or other decorative elements. A mesh background carries a design that can be laid into any type of flooring, though stone is most common. A classic Greek key, curling waves, vines, or autumn leaves might form the edge of a simple stone floor. With planning and preparation, you might also insert a mosaic decorative element into a ceramic tile or even wood floor, to become part of an overall material mix for the ultimate personal flooring statement.

You might use mosaics to create a colorful picture in the center of a kitchen floor, for example. A mosaic in the same color stone as an entry floor might scribe the initials of the homeowners for a subtle yet highly personal statement. Or consider the drama created when a glass mosaic element is introduced into honed marble; the reflective mosaic glitters like a jewel in the rich, matte surface. There really are no limitations; mosaics are as comfortable on a bathroom floor as they are in a formal living room.

Just as you can enrich an outfit with well-chosen accessories, so too can a floor be ornamented with mosaics. But stone pictures have more versatility than clothing accessories; they can take center stage to star in the dramatic composition. Few floors make as powerful a design statement as those whose entire surface is composed of colorful bits of stone. Consider mosaics as a flooring material if you want hardness and longevity combined with color and finely detailed pattern.

Above: Insert a mosaic border for a rich, luxurious statement. Such borders are now available as separate elements; they can be placed at the whim of the floor designer.

Left: Pretty pictures composed with small, colored stones—that's what mosaics are all about.

Mosaic Motifs

Mosaic Florals and Foliage

Mosaic Borders

Tile Style

For many rooms, tile is a beautiful and practical choice. When it comes to tile, ceramic is the classic. It cleans easily, is very durable, and is resistant to dampness. This makes it ideal for kitchens and baths, as well as vestibules and foyers—which may see a bit of water, snow, and mud during wet weather. But ceramic tile is only the beginning. What about vinyl, leather, cork, wood, concrete, plastic, and even glass? Following are some exciting ways to use tile in your home.

- Mix ceramic tiles with abandon. For a Mediterranean atmosphere, complement earthy terra-cotta tiles with a border of hand-painted or Mexican tiles for a unique blend of old-world flavor.

- Colored glass tiles give floors a subtle yet distinctive glow, and since they're made from bits of recycled glass, they will impress your environmentally conscious guests. You don't need to outfit a whole room in glass tile. Try them in a border treatment around a more traditional ceramic tile bathroom floor.

- Stone tiles—brick, slate, limestone, marble, and other natural materials—are perfect for low-maintenance, high-interest flooring in kitchens, baths, and even living rooms.

- Install colorful vinyl tiles in a checkerboard pattern to liven up a retro-styled kitchen. Vinyl tiles are an easy way for the do-it-yourselfer on a budget to give a room an entirely new look. Softer, less expensive, and easier to install than its ceramic, marble, and stone cousins, vinyl tile is manufactured in a wide variety of colors, patterns, and textures.

- Concrete tiles can be tinted to match countertops, cabinetry, even your favorite set of china, and they look great with today's restaurant-inspired kitchens. They're also durable and extremely low maintenance—an occasional damp-mopping will keep them looking stunning.

- Indulge in leather tiles to lend an air of sophistication to less traffic-heavy spaces. A rich leather floor can become the focal point of a living room, bedroom, or study. ■ ■ ■

Vinyl Composition Tile

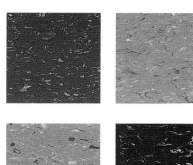

Vinyl Composition Tile

Indian Ivory Limestone Tile

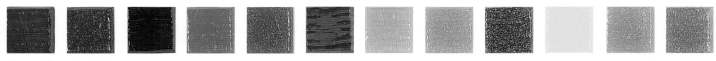

Vitreous Glass Mosaic Tile

Leather Floor and Wall Tile

Tile with the hand-thrown look of pottery works to create a dimensional field of color and soft pattern.

Linoleum Style

Linoleum, the first thoroughly modern flooring material, is the darling flooring of today's animal-rights activists and environmentalists. It is entirely made of natural, renewable materials: linseed oil, wood flour, ground cork, limestone, jute. It's handsome and comfortable. A bonus is the characteristic smell, which is the faint aroma of the flax seed or linseed oil—that's at the heart of this lovely product.

Linoleum was eclipsed by vinyl as a favorite flooring for much of the past fifty years, but it's making a strong comeback. Recent introductions of both jute and polyester-backed linoleum tile have brought about something new—do-it-yourself linoleum installation. It's tougher than vinyl; the curing process of linoleum continues long after installation, so that it gets harder and more durable with age.

Today's decorators favor linoleum in marbled and flecked solids, pieced to make graphic color and design statements. It's easy to cut, thus suiting it to smooth curves that aren't possible with most materials. Early color limitations have been largely eliminated, as have some of the more lurid florals of the past. Floor borders and corners are available as stock items in geometrics and classic motifs.

Linoleum is great in kitchens—comfortable for the cook, durable, and easy to clean. But don't think of it as merely utilitarian. Linoleum is good-looking, and can go wherever you want it to. ▧ ■ ▨

Left: Linoleum has astonishing longevity. Chic again, it has come full circle in our style sensibility. Along with that comes new appreciation for the old patterns.

Linoleum Options

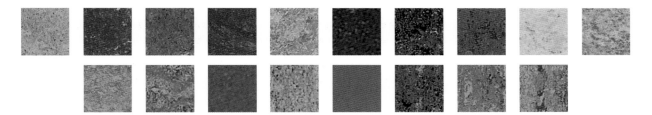

Single-layer linoleum comes in a beautiful range of colors.

Marbled, flecked, and graphic patterns are newly popular.

Vinyl Style

With vinyl, floors entered the twentieth century. One hundred years later, it is solidly entrenched as a flooring favorite. Resilient, available at every price point in a vast array of colors and patterns, easy to install and care for—vinyl is truly for every home.

Because of its dominance in the flooring market, vinyl sheet or tile can be found to suit any style of interior. Contemporary manufacturing processes now use extreme heat and pressure to sculpt the surface of the material, producing texture for a particular design feature such as the grout of a tile or the pebbled surface of a stone design. Realistic visual appeal combined with vinyl's smooth resilience makes this the choice for homeowners who want the look for less combined with easy care. At the high end of the price spectrum, sheet vinyl floors are subtly colored and lavishly cushioned. And, keep in mind that vinyl tile flooring is easily installed by do-it-yourselfers.

A recent vinyl flooring introduction comes from Sweden, where it is used as the raw material for a woven wall-to-wall carpet. Vinyl fibers, which resemble the gimp you made lanyards from at summer camp, are machine-woven for a tough top layer, which is then bonded to a vinyl base. The result has greater texture and is softer than vinyl sheet or tile. It is extremely strong, water-resistant, and has the surface of woven fabric, but without the nap. It is available either in bold stripes of color, or in the tweeds created by two colors woven together.

At the high end, a vinyl floor costing as much as cork or wood can incorporate extra cushioning and sound-absorption features, along with designer patterns and colors. Most vinyl flooring is priced in the low and middle range. But designers newly enamored of vinyls and laminates (aka plastics) create across the board. There is very chic, very affordable vinyl flooring: Investigate 12-inch by 12-inch (30 cm by 30 cm) self-adhesive floor tiles in pale neutral shades, for instance.

The wildly popular wood laminate floor is, in fact, a close relative of vinyl flooring. The material has come a long way; vinyl flooring is a direct descendant of Bakelite, the first completely synthetic plastic, introduced in 1909. It was made and marketed during the early twentieth century as Vinylite. ▬ ■ ▬

Vinyl Options

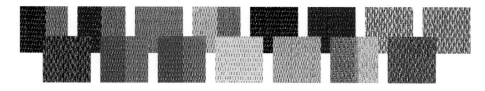

Woven vinyl has a great texture and iron-clad durability.

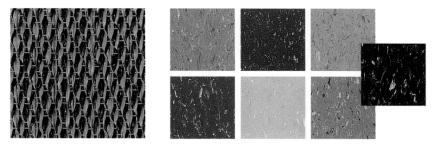

Vinyl Composition Tile

Vinyl flooring can look like anything and go anywhere. At its best, it is so much a part of a room that nothing else could be imagined in its place.

Soft Flooring
Options

We have a craving for softness under our feet, especially in our homes. Soft flooring is easy on the back while we're standing, and it gives us visual cues that say "comfort." We can expect to keep seeing new developments until the possibilities of nearly every kind of material have been exhausted—and that won't happen as long as artists and designers keep having ideas.

Carpeting pile presents problems for allergy sufferers, but sometimes a vinyl floor just isn't natural enough. From Finland comes the Verso carpet. Linen fabric, which is extremely strong, is woven through birch slats, with the two materials forming the warp and the woof of the carpet. The results look like a hand-woven cotton or wool rug, with the protruding ends of the birch slats forming the fringe. Since the birch elements are extremely thin, the carpeting has much more flexibility than you'd expect. Patterns have a bold Scandinavian look that's perfect for modern interiors or for folkloric design schemes.

Leather tiles make a floor that's comfortable, atmospheric, and surprisingly long wearing. Now, a new line of leather flooring tile has brought color. Aniline dyes, far-removed from the shoe-polish-like leather stains of the past, produce saturated colors like terra-cotta reds, forest greens, ochre yellows, as well as more traditional oxblood and saddle colors. A great choice for libraries or dens, leather flooring is moving into bedrooms, where its sound-absorption is especially appreciated. ■ ■ ■

Left: Cork is perennially among our favorites for soft flooring; painting or stenciling it adds whole new design possibilities.

Right: Carpets are always in vogue but can always look new.

Beautiful Bamboo

Think of the design potential of a bamboo floor. The perennial grass favored by pandas, bamboo encompasses a huge family of plants, some of which are ideal for flooring. While strong (it looks like hardwood), bamboo flooring has the pale coloration we associate with this plant, as well as the characteristic protruded ringed joints, known as knuckles. The effect is perfectly suited to an Asian-inspired interior, or to a design scheme that seeks to emphasize natural materials. Environmentalists are especially fond of bamboo for flooring because it is a renewable resource.

The latest evolution in bamboo flooring is an engineered product called plyboo, in which wood laminates are faced with a top wear layer of bamboo. It is not inexpensive and makes a versatile product.

Left: Leather flooring, beautiful and fragrant, is surprisingly tough.

Right: The sound-deadening characteristics of leather floor tiles make them especially popular in bedrooms, living rooms, or anywhere else where quiet, luxury, and softness are appreciated.

A Range in Leather

Defining Space
with Flooring

Floors are unique. They do double duty as structural and as decorative parts of a home. As such, they must be designed around your needs and wishes. Floor designers will often focus on the floor's structural strength to the exclusion of other important considerations. Once you know what your many design options are, you can work with your designer to get a floor that is structurally sound and aesthetically pleasing.

Use your floors to define space. Once you start to think outside the limits of floors as background, you open up design possibilities that can improve the function of the rooms in your house. People automatically set their feet on the flooring that appears to be most comfortable and stable; use this knowledge consciously, and your home's traffic patterns will make sense, regardless of the size of the living area.

An often-mentioned problem for modern homeowners is a cramped entrance to their homes. If your floor leads the eye into an adjoining room, perhaps flowing in and becoming a part of it, a small entryway will seem larger.

Sometimes the opposite creates a problem—an open expanse of floor leaves visitors without directional signals; they literally don't know which way to turn. Think of this as an opportunity to use pattern. By creating visual pathways, you'll lead guests in the direction you'd like them to go. ■ ■ ■

Of course, structural strength is important; combined with beauty, it makes the best floor.

Top Left: Once you think outside of predictable parameters, you can use floors to define space in exciting ways.

Top Right: A small entry can be visually enlarged through the use of the right flooring.

Bottom Left: Give visual and tactile clues to those entering your home.

Botton Right: How a floor feels and sounds are part of what helps determine traffic patterns.

Tactile sensations send equally important signals. A smooth, resilient floor that changes to a softer carpet underfoot shows us the boundaries between the kitchen's areas of use; the cook stands on the smooth floor while guests congregate in the cozy corner. Similarly, a carpet defines the conversation area in a living room with polished marble floors. In these cases, form follows function—the carpet protects the mirrorlike surface of the stone and the business end of the kitchen is easy to clean.

Two types of flooring material signal change in use as well as visually separating space.

Choose your materials with thought. The simplest element can make a strong statement on the floor; you need not spend a large amount of money to produce an interesting and imaginative effect. When nailing down soft pine boards, for instance, you might space the nails in a pattern, or you might precolor the wood plugs that are commonly used to cover them. The result can be compelling: Imagine a wide-board softwood floor, with its characteristic knots and color variations, marked with a grid of blue dots. Needless to say, the plugs (boatbuilders call them bungs) will be most effective if they echo the room's architecture, play up a color scheme, or lead the eye toward a focal point or into the next room.

A modern kitchen is up a set of marble steps; in the kitchen, the floor changes to wood.

Does your new house look a little too new? The single best way to give it that lived-in atmosphere is with flooring. Explore the varieties of recycled old floorboards now on the market. Older flooring often comes in wide widths, a feature appreciated by many homeowners. A number of companies offer the floors that were once in industrial buildings, but some of this type of flooring comes from more exotic places. Pine logs that have spent 150 years submerged in riverbeds, for instance, are the source for a particularly lovely patinated wood floorboard.

Top: The dining room of a
brand new house achieves
the gentle patina of age
through the use of old,
recycled floorboards.

Left: Material creates
atmosphere. Here, metal
stairs make a space that is
streamlined, spare, open,
and modern.

Top: Classic does not mean dull. Imaginative flooring will look good in the long term while remaining stylish.

Left: Think it through; your favorite, most personal way of creating an interior includes the floor.

Floors Last a Lifetime

Keep one thing in mind: Your floors should last for the life of the house, and you may tire of any overtly trendy flooring statement long before its natural life is over. You will also want to give some consideration to possible future changes in décor. This is not to say that your floors should be neutral, dull 'go with everything' compromises. Some of the most beautiful, classic flooring options are also the most versatile. But, if you install a floor composed of large limestone slabs, for example, it is unlikely that you'll want to replace it. If you get tired of it, which is also unlikely, the best you'll be able to do is to cover it with something.

A carefully considered floor isn't one you'll want or need to re-do periodically. Design your floor for the long term, and it will give you renewed pleasure every day.

No matter how small, a carpet can create an area entirely separate from the rest of the room. Here is a small oasis for rest and reflection.

For the most direct and delightful flooring experiences, walking and talking have it all over showrooms. So we sought out a few people responsible for flooring we especially admired. Gather inspiration from their style ideas in the pages that follow, and make it your own.

Section 4
Style File

Style File

Not that their flooring choices have much in common, beside the obvious fact that each homeowner, designer, business, and craftsperson strove for flooring that was true to the home's overall philosophy and aesthetic. But, oh, what variety we see! There's stone, certainly to be expected as a personal choice among the design and flooring cognoscenti. But here we see stone in a rainbow of color from white to ocher yellow to dark red to black, in shapes ranging from small chunks to expansive slabs to finely detailed pictures, and then there are the finishes—and that's traveling to only two of the five homes shown! There is VCT (vinyl composition tile), flooring so universally available that it's often taken for granted, yet it is ever so stylish in a house with very specific stylistic demands. Look at how an architect who wanted a floor with energy efficiency, affordability, toughness, and progressive good looks combined all of those with stained concrete. At the opposite end of the spectrum, a weekend getaway for collectors of important Asian art is the right place for exotic, delicate bamboo. And wood, that familiar and beloved flooring material, is taken to new heights by a homeowner whose design and flooring experts understood her love of nature in all its flowering glory. ■ ■ ■

Touchstone
Flooring

What kind of flooring does a top name in the business install for herself? We asked Ann Sacks, of the namesake company, and found that years of intimacy with the subject have directed her choices toward timeless beauty married to sophisticated, modern technology.

For twenty years, Ann Sacks has been providing homeowners with an ever-increasing variety of beautiful surfacing materials. Ann Sacks, the company, started when Ann Sacks, the woman, was shopping for a dress in Portland, Oregon. The shop had a small display of Mexican tiles that caught her interest, and within a short time Ann Sacks was no longer a special-needs teacher but, rather, an entrepreneur. She started the Custom Color Tile program, a concept that seems eminently sensible now, but was unheard-of at the time.

"We matched tiles to whatever—you could bring us a sample of fabric, or a wall color, anything, and we'd make tiles to match," she explains.

Throughout the eighties, Ann Sacks built a solid reputation for beautiful and innovative tile in a field where products were either beautiful or innovative, but never both. Her products were at the forefront of the Arts and Crafts revival; when collectors furnished their homes with the newly pricey Mission oak antiques, Ann Sacks tiles created a sympathetic backdrop. When a craze for luxury spa baths swept the United States during the 1990s, her products were the connoisseur's choice to create polished stone temples to self-indulgence. Today, Ann Sacks furnishes the country with a vast variety of tile, stone, and mosaics, as well as a new line of bathroom fixtures and furnishings. Ann Sacks, the company, is now a subsidiary of Kohler but is still very clearly in the hands of Ann Sacks, the woman.

So when this energetic, forward-looking woman recently rehabilitated a downtown Portland industrial building to serve as company headquarters, with housing for her family and herself on the top two floors, she installed heated limestone slab floors there.

"They are luxurious and beautiful," she says, "but truly forever."

The flooring surface is composed of large Italian limestone slabs in a warm, ocherlike color known as Princess Yellow. Under-floor radiant heat makes it cozy.

"It's very simple technology," Ann points out. "It's attached to the hot-water system." She speaks with passion about stone as a flooring material.

"It imparts a sense of luxury and is going to look more beautiful in twenty-five years than it does now. Stone is the only material that's more beautiful with time. The increased value of a home with stone floors is great."

A wood and metal dining room table surrounded by Breuer chairs rest beautifully on Ann Sacks' limestone slab flooring.

Ann Sacks on advances in stone production: "Equipment that's been developed in Europe has made cutting and polishing faster and less labor-intensive for beautifully calibrated, thinner tiles. It has revolutionized the industry so that now we have thin, uniform stone. In our business we're going in the direction of sleek, great design, and there's nothing like a slab stone floor for that."

Stone slabs can be used to create nearly seamless surfaces, as opposed to tiles, where the surface is necessarily broken up with many seams. With careful planning, sections where slabs join can be placed so that they are hidden under furniture, or minimized in out-of-the-way areas. As a result, the pattern in the stone takes center stage.

"This stone has so much of a pattern that it looks like it moves," Ann Sacks laughs. She clearly loves her beautiful new floors.

This stone has so much of a pattern that appears to move. The larger the piece of stone, the more pronounced its natural markings.

The color of Ann's flooring coordinates with her furnishings in every room, including the bathroom.

Something New:
Bamboo

In a high-rise condominium far above the beach, a Miami interior designer created an Asian-inspired decorating scheme. Components of the design include a rich red wall color resembling cinnabar, important Asian art, a curved wall built to resemble a shoji screen, and the liberal use of bamboo. Bamboo covers the floor throughout the home. It is also applied to the ceilings in "floating" panels that define space and introduce visual complexity, and bamboo lines parts of several walls.

"It's a very dense, very strong material," says Dennis Jenkins, the designer responsible for this project. "For flooring, it comes in $1/4$-inch (.5 cm) strips, and it looks a lot like hardwood, only it's lighter in color than wood floors tend to be. I definitely chose it for its relevance to the overall design. An Asian theme calls for it."

Bamboo's paleness, plus its characteristic ringed joints, generally referred to as knees or knuckles, usually give it an unmistakable look as a flooring material. But at first (and second) glance, this floor could easily pass for herringbone-patterned wood parquet. There are no knees to give it away; the strips of bamboo are short, therefore cut between the rings, and look similar to clear hardwood ("Clear" wood indicates that it was milled and cut so that the usable planks or strips display no knotholes.) The overall effect is serene yet rich, with pale color flowing in a uniform surface throughout the apartment. As with much Asian design, the complexity of the pattern is not evident right away, and each design element subtly reinforces the theme. In this contemporary fusion of Asian and American second-home design, the overall effect is modern, serene, and very sophisticated. Although the condominium measures about 2,000 square feet (186 square meters) overall, it appears larger. A lot of the responsibility for the illusion of much more space goes to the unbroken expanse of flooring.

This seasonal home is sophisticated and uncluttered but comfortable nonetheless.

Elegant, but Fragile

Dennis Jenkins does, however, point out bamboo's limitations as a flooring material. He indicates that he would not recommend bamboo floors for commercial applications.

Carefully chosen Asian art is part of the design scheme.

"As a flooring material, it's fragile," he says. "It could not take the heavy wear of public places or of high-traffic areas. Nor would I have recommended it if this unit were on the ground floor, where sand was constantly being tracked in from the beach. In this instance, it's perfect." This particular condominium unit, high above the beach, is a secondary residence; as a weekend and vacation home, it does not bear the level of foot traffic the owners' primary residence does.

But here, in an interior designed around a yen for something different, elegant, and Far East in flavor, bamboo makes a lovely floor.

Top Left: In this condominium unit, bamboo is used for flooring and on the walls and ceiling.

Top Right: Bamboo on the floor and in floating ceiling panels helps create the illusion of an expanse of space.

Bottom Left: High above the beach, this floor works. On the ground floor, it might be subject to constantly tracked-in sand, which would ruin it.

Bottom Right: Serene, pale, and modern are this home's keynotes.

DESIGN SPECIFICATIONS

MATERIALS: $1/4$-inch (.5cm) strip bamboo
AREA COVERED: 2,000 square feet

DESIGNER: Dennis Jenkins Interior Design Associates
5813 South West 68th Street
Miami, FL 33143
(305) 665-6960

INSTALLED BY: Carpet Creations
7310 Southwest 45th Street
Miami, FL 33155

Spanish
Colonial

"It's too bad the floors had been done so inappropriately," Desiree Caskill says. "But then, if they hadn't been, we wouldn't have had the opportunity to do this!"

"This" is a floor of rare beauty, where classic marble mosaics alternate with inlaid pebble-stone, honed marble paving blocks, and large limestone tiles. The different shapes, sizes, and varieties of inlaid stone create large geometric patterns in earth tones of red, white and gold that bring life to the huge expanse of living room floor. It is a fitting ground for a magnificent room.

When Desiree, the principal of Casa Mia Design, was growing up, she walked by this house every day.

"I thought it was so beautiful," she recalls. "I'd be on my way home from school, and I'd stop at the corner and look, thinking that this was what Florida must have been like at one time—quiet, lush, historic looking."

If not exemplifying the whole state, then at one time this town certainly did resemble an oasis. Coral Gables was an early planned community, built during the 1920s by George Merrick. Into his plans he incorporated parkways, landscaped plazas, gateways built of coral, and royal poinciana trees, many of which survive to this day. Early on in that process, this house was built of steel-reinforced concrete on a large corner lot. It was considered quite an architectural feat for its time: In 1926, the *Miami Herald* claimed that there were no other houses like it. Years later it certainly was uniquely attractive to Desiree, who grew up admiring the house as a superb example of the architectural style that is so dear to Florida's historic heart, Spanish Colonial Revival. The house style of choice during the state's 1920s real estate boom is represented in genteel pockets of early twentieth-century development throughout Florida's older cities. Hallmarks include thick walls of stucco or earthenwork, palladian windows, clay tile roofs, second-story loggias (columned and arcaded balconies), and fancy iron grillwork. The big house on the corner seemed to have it all.

Desiree Caskill and her husband were house hunting in nearby Miami when, in a Dickensian twist of wish fulfillment, this house was placed on the market. The first time her husband saw it, he was smitten.

And so he and Desiree came to own the home she'd admired years ago. She had become an interior designer with particular knowledge about Spanish Colonial Revival interiors. It was clear that some of the alterations that had been made over the years had not been kind.

"Whoever had owned it before us had put down new floors—originally, they would have been stone—and had laid monochromatic tiles throughout the house. They were dark and made the rooms look gloomy, as well as featureless," Desiree explains. "Small, repeating squares just exaggerated the expanse of floor, especially in the living room."

A geometric floor composed of limestone and marble in a variety of colors and shapes makes a formal floor for a magnificent room.

A Unified Scheme

The living room is anchored at one end by a tall, arched window overlooking the garden. A carved-stone fireplace is centered on one of the long walls. Opposite, doorways lead to other rooms and to staircases. With a high coffered ceiling that was beautifully painted when the house was first built, the room has the formality and presence of a medieval reception hall but the warmth and personality of a family great room. The inlaid floor not only reflects the regular patterning of the ceiling but also echoes its muted colors. The paler tones of the floor are also seen in the carved stone of the fireplace surround.

A remnant of the original flooring was found in the foyer. It served as a springboard for design inspiration.

That served as one cue to the restoration process. Another was in the entry hall, where a small portion of the original floor had survived. A magnificent mosaic forms a compass rose pattern against a background of pale limestone. This lovely old floor seamlessly leads into the living room, with its lovely new floor.

By putting back what might have been there originally, Desiree Caskill has brought back color and pattern, and the room now has a unified decorative scheme that it had lost over time.

DESIGN SPECIFICATIONS

MATERIALS: Limestone and marble tiles in various shapes and sizes.

TILE: Waterworks
29 Park Avenue
Danbury, CT 06810
(800) 899-6757

DESIGN: Casa Mia Design
P.O. Box 140817
Coral Gables, FL 33114
(305) 569-0529

The light-colored stone of the fireplace surround helped dictate the floor's restoration.

The Green House

Like many architects, Ted Montgomery is an idealist. As a husband and father designing and building his family's home, however, he was grounded in the realities of budget and Vermont winters. This doesn't mean that he had to compromise; especially when it came to his floors, he acted on both his idealism and his practicality. A favored contemporary flooring material, stained concrete, met his specifications for good looking, affordable, and environmentally friendly floors. Installing radiant heat beneath it made it warm. Its avant-garde chic may not have been his first reason for choosing it, but it's true that stained concrete has been growing in popularity among architects, designers, and cutting-edge interior decorators. The smooth, beautifully colored surfaces are waxed to produce a finish that has guests wondering just what that really is under their feet.

"We call it Montgomery Marble," Ted laughs. The floor is organically mottled in shades of red and green and could easily be mistaken for an exotic and expensive stone. Instead, it is the flooring material so practical and economical that it is standard for industrial applications. However, the way Ted and his wife finished the concrete gives it great beauty while retaining qualities of longevity, heat retention, simplicity of installation, ease of maintenance, and economy. What's more, the Montgomerys did it themselves.

The process was relatively simple, though it took a while. Once the poured concrete floor was finished, with hoses for the heating system installed underneath and the surface troweled to a smooth finish, it was allowed to cure for six months. When all the moisture had evaporated and the material was stable, the Montgomerys applied the stain, which is actually an acid that etches the surface of the concrete.

"We had been seeing some of this etched concrete in architectural and design circles, but this was the first time we'd tried it for ourselves. We chose a color called Bronze for its red and green component, but we really had no idea how it was going to turn out."

The results were delightful, though not entirely predictable.

"We mopped the stuff on," Ted explains. "It fizzed ever so slightly as it was working."

The result turned out to be much more dramatic than anticipated, with colors forming eddies and rivulets in the concrete. Ted decided to help the process along by moving the colors around with a long-handled mop to form large, swirling color variations.

"Four hours later we washed it off. Then we washed it again, and applied a water-based sealant. The whole process was fairly simple, though it took a few days."

Delicious Warmth

"The under-floor radiant heat, which runs off bottled gas, works like a charm. The house heats quite well, with 50 percent humidity even during the winters, when everything usually dries out so terribly. It's very comfortable. The floor actually doesn't feel warm to the touch, except in spots on very cold days, when the system is cranking at top capacity." The mass of the poured concrete floor acts to retain heat. Together with the passive solar gain of the Montgomerys' garden room; their Vermont Castings woodstove; and a new, energy-efficient parlor fireplace, they meet the challenge of staying warm during icy northern winters without excessive cost or environmental degradation.

The Montgomery's etched-concrete floor is part of an overall design of energy efficiency.

"The floor is a perfect heat sink," Ted explains. But even while he was becoming convinced that he had made the right decision from an environmental and economical point of view, he wasn't so sure about the floor's aesthetics over the long run.

"It took us two years to gather up the courage to apply a coat of wax. When we did, it gave it a lovely sheen and made it look brand new again. We thought the wax might make the floor too slippery, but that was only true where water was spilled."

What had given the Montgomerys the impetus to renew their floor was an impending magazine story—their home has become a cause celèbre in the community of environmental activists.

Despite its exotic appearance, this is a tough floor that's up to the demands of a busy family.

Etched concrete makes a practical surface for a kitchen floor.

"We've been in magazines, and on TV; our house is becoming well known. And when a photographer is due, we wax the floor a bit and it looks gorgeous again. A commonly available commercial liquid wax does the trick."

Like well-designed houses everywhere, the Montgomery home is all of a piece and suited to its site; the design and construction form a coherent whole. It's a comfortable and personal place for a family and an efficient system to produce and conserve energy. The floors are an integral part of both those aspects—and they're lovely to boot.

"We love the way the floors work," Ted Montgomery says. "And when people walk in and see them for the first time, what they usually say is, 'Wow!'"

This member of the family especially likes the radiant heat.

This floor is not only tough and energy efficient, it is also beautiful and modern.

Flowers
Underfoot

Floors are functional, yes, but there's a floor in a South Florida condominium that proves that the most practical of walking surfaces can also be fine art. On this floor, a flowering vine seems to grow out of the hardwood strips in the foyer. It makes its way through a gate that leads into the rooms of the house and continues curling in and out of corners, petals blowing before the breeze coming in from a terrace, turning toward the sun before a window, until it wends its way through every room and back to where it started. It looks delicate, ephemeral, even, but it's every bit as sturdy as the rock-hard maple that forms the background to this delightful floral mosaic.

The floor is the result of a happy three-way collaboration between the home's owner, her decorator, and a flooring professional. The owner provided the design inspiration by suggesting that her new home bring nature inside with a plant motif. Interior designer Dalia Berlin came up with the idea of a flowering vine in a hardwood floor. Finally, Leonard A. Hall spent six weeks on his hands and knees, bringing it to life.

None of this creative partnership would have been possible if today's world of wood flooring were not light-years ahead of where it was a few years ago. Laser-cutting technology now makes it easier to produce finely detailed shapes perfectly each time, and state-of-the-art-bonding materials keep it all together. But this was by no means an automatic process.

Lenny Hall, a flooring contractor, explains that he had never done something free-form like this, not in a repeating pattern. "It was an incredible experience to be able to do something that involved so much workmanship and creativity," he says. "I literally drew this vine out on the floor and then built it in wood. In all, there are 145 feet (44.2 m) of wall line with a totally free-hand vine."

"It's very organic," Dalia Berlin says. This floor was a first for her, as well. "I've done a few projects like this since, but only borders. This was something special." She goes on to explain that when her client wanted to "bring nature indoors," it meant going far beyond the usual flowered drapes or botanical prints. The floor, as the most basic element in a home's design, proved a surprising but essential place to incorporate nature so that its images were not merely decorative accents but part of the structure itself.

For the main floor, Lenny Hall laid 3 $^1/_4$-inch-wide (8.9 cm) maple boards from Canada. As a wood species, maple is exceptionally hard, but Lenny's primary reason for this choice is maple's suitability as a background. He explains that it's not like other commonly used types of hardwood flooring; you don't see a lot of heavy graining or different colors from board to board, as you would with oak. "That would have played havoc with the fine lines of this design," he says.

He sketched the vine onto the maple background, but did some homework before he began. "I took some time to study books on botany. Not only had I never drawn a completely free-hand design like this, but I didn't know flowers very well. First I made a mock-up, a three-foot sample. Now, when I look at it, I cringe, but the homeowner saw the potential in it and gave me carte blanche."

"I hand picked the materials so that the grain and coloration would work as part of the design. Flower petals are made of American cherry, Honduran mahogany, Santos mahogany, bubinga, lacewood, Brazilian cherry, and padauk. The flower centers are the same maple as the background. The vine itself is made of number two poplar. It's from the heart of the tree, and is naturally a green color—perfect for a vine."

A flowering vine starts in a small private foyer, in front of a hand-tiled wall.

The hand-carved elements, made up of nine different wood species, are not merely glued to the top like veneer. The vine is an integral part of the floor, going through the whole thickness of the tongue-and-groove maple boards. It can be sanded and refinished without endangering the design. The entire creation was finished in a protective layer of polyurethane, which was then sanded and covered with a final water-based matte finish, also polyurethane.

As it passes through the gates into the apartment, the vine separates and heads in two directions towards rooms on either side.

The free-form wood picture incorporates whimsical elements. Three ladybugs are hidden in the foliage, composed of padauk and wenge. An ash, purple heart, and wenge butterfly flits across a section of floor. Where the vine crosses the area in front of a sliding door to a balcony, the flowers appear to be wind blown, their petals turned and tossed in the ocean breezes. Yet, for all its delicacy, it's as tough as wooden floors come.

The homeowner explains that lots of holidays have been celebrated here, with children running and grownups wearing party shoes. "The floor is very practical," she says. "It is not fragile, it has not been protected, but it looks beautiful. Nothing has been done to it except that it's been walked on a lot."

This enterprise was so successful that it won the National Wood Flooring Association's Floor of the Year award. It has lead to other projects for both Lenny Hall and Dalia Berlin, though both claim that this floor is not only the first but also the best of its kind they've ever done.

The way the homeowner feels about it is evidenced by an unusual step she just took. Presently building a larger home, she has specified that future buyers of this condominium must give Lenny the opportunity to come and remove it if they do not want the floor.

"Then he can use it in his showroom," she explains. "It is his creation—he should be able to show it off."

Lenny smiles and acknowledges this. But he can't believe that anyone would not want this floor as part of their home.

Indeed, it's hard to imagine.

With its sweet flowers and curling tendrils, this may look like a delicate floor. It is anything but.

DESIGN SPECIFICATIONS

MATERIAL: Nine varieties of wood

DESIGNER: Dalia Berlin, ASID
Berlin Design, Inc.
3511 Greenleaf Circle
Hollywood, FL 33021
(954) 967-6576

INSTALLATION: Leonard A. Hall
Endurance Flooring Company Inc.
18460 N.E. 2nd Ave.
Miami, FL 33179
(305) 652-6481

The Ralph
and Sunny Wilson
House

Here's a flooring irony.

In the home of a pioneering laminate king, there's no laminate flooring. And then, when the house was remodeled years later by the company he started, they still didn't put in any laminate flooring. In fact, the original and replacement floor tiles in Ralph and Sunny Wilson's house weren't—and aren't—even Wilsonart products.

His ranch-style house house in Temple, Texas, came on the market nearly fifty years after Ralph Wilson built it. Wilsonart, the laminate giant he started, bought the house in 1998, and restored it to a 1950s décor under the direction of New York decorator Grace Jeffers. It is now open to the public as a house museum.

When Wilsonart bought it, the house was structurally sound, part of its eye-popping appeal. No one had built a house like this before: Ralph Wilson had used laminate in unheard-of new places, including as wall material placed directly over studs. On the kitchen countertops he experimented with postforming, a process where laminate is bent to form continuous curves from the top to the side edge of the counter. Laminate-clad cabinetry was installed in the kitchen, laundry, and bathrooms, and shower walls were laminate. These are all commonplace installations today, but were unheard-of in the late fifties. But here it was, 1998, and the walls looked just as they were built to look in 1959.

The original furniture was long gone, and Grace Jeffers replaced it with classic 1950s Moderne pieces by Eero Saarinen and Charles and Ray Eames, among others.

DESIGN SPECIFICATIONS

MATERIALS: Armstrong 9-inch by 9-inch (23 cm by 23 cm) Vinyl Composition Tile

DESIGN: Grace Jeffers

HOUSE INFORMATION: The Ralph and Sunny Wilson House
Temple, TX 76501
(254) 773-9898

As for the floors—they were in good shape, too. They were the latest thing in 1959 flooring—vinyl asbestos tile. For reasons of safety, Wilsonart and Jeffers decided to replaced the floor tiles in the kitchen and dining room with vinyl composition tile by Armstrong. The living room had carpeting but is now surfaced with an aqua vinyl composition tile that unifies the original aqua colors in the laminate kitchen cabinetry. The original floor remains in two bathrooms, where it has been deemed safe. It is peach-tinged in one bathroom, pink and gray in the other. Each is banded with blue strips. The pink and gray tile was original to the kitchen as well, and the blue-banded tile is the same, old and new.

The Wilson House has traveled far since Ralph Wilson built it on its Temple, Texas, lot. He wanted it to serve as his private residence, a model home for his fledgling company, and as a site to test the quality and durability of his products. As august a body as the National Register of Historic Places agrees that he succeeded. They named the Wilson House to its register, naming it as a significant architectural structure.

So why isn't there any laminate flooring in the historic home of the laminate king? When he built his house, it hadn't been invented yet. Then, when the house was remodeled, Grace Jeffers chose floor tiles that were close to the originals. But we can't help but think that, if laminate floors had been invented, Ralph Wilson would have used them in his house. In fact, it's surprising that he didn't invent them!

Top Left: Laminate walls installed in the 1959 living room still provide a graphic exclamation point.

Left: There is laminate throughout the house—but not on the floor.

Center and Right: Replacement vinyl floor tiles in the kitchen, and the originals in the bathroom (right).

The New
Flooring Idea Book

Creating Style from the Ground Up

Carolyn L. Bates
Carolyn L. Bates Photography
P.O. Box 1205
Burlington, VT 05402
(802) 862-5386
www.carolynbates.com
pp. 17, 19, 31, 34, 37 (middle right), 48 (left), 71
(top left), 96, 97 (top), 117, 118, 119, 120, 121

Brian Vanden Brink, Photographer
P. O. Box 419
Rockport, ME 04856
pp. 16, 24, 25, 26, 37 (top right, middle left, lower left & right)
41, 45 (top left & middle, bottom right), 48 (middle), 71 (top &
bottom right), 73 (bottom left),77, 85, 93, 94 (top left & bottom), 95, 97 (bottom), 98 (top)

Scott Dorrance
Scott Dorrance Studio, Inc.,
142 High Street
Portland, ME 04101
(207) 772-1811
pp. 15, 45 (top right & bottom left)

Elizabeth Whiting Associates
70 Mornington Street
London, NW1 7QD England
Dennis Stone p. 51
Mark Luscombe p. 52
Graham Henderson p. 83

Bruce Martin
Bruce T. Martin Photography
17 Tudor Street
Cambridge, MA 02139
(617) 492-8009
p. 59 (left)

Willig/Alberts/Picture Press
Hamburg, Germany
p. 40

Willig/Picture Press
Hamburg, Germany
p. 87, 99

Hajo Willig/Picture Press
Hamburg, Germany
p. 89 (left)

Ivo Nörenberg/Picture Press
Hamburg, Germany
p. 89 (right)

Willig/Lichtenstein/Picture Press
Hamburg, Germany
p. 55

Hefe/Report Bilder-Dienst GmbH
Munich, Germany
p. 56

Dietrich/Report Bilder-Dienst GmbH
Munich, Germany
p. 20, 63 (left)

Hoernisch/Report Bilder-Deinst GmbH
Munich, Germany
p. 61

Beateworks/
Tim Street-Porter
2400 S. Shenandoah Street
Los Angeles, CA 90034
p. 27

Greg Premru
Greg Premru Photography
345 Congress Street
Boston, MA 02210
(617) 451-7770
p. 59 (right)

Lanny Provo, Photographer
10980 NW 10 Street
Plantation, Florida 33322
(954) 424-3143
pp. 29, 48 (right), 49 (top), 90, 103 (top right, middle, bottom right), 109, 110, 111, 113, 114, 115, 123, 124, 125

Red Cover/Winfried Heinze
1 Swans Mews
London SW6 4QT, England
p. 73 (top & bottom right)

Red Cover/Christopher Drake
1 Swans Mews
London SW6 4QT, England
p. 94 (top right)

Red Cover/Graham Atkins-Hughes
1 Swans Mews
London SW6 4QT, England
p. 34 (right), p. 96 (top right), 98 (bottom)

Through the Lens Management, Inc.
4111 C Marathon Blvd.
Austin, TX 78756
(512) 302-9391
Greg Hursley p. 21
Paul Bardagjy pp. 23, 28, 39, 103 (bottom left), 127

Peter A. Sellar
Peter Sellar Photography
2403 Fourth Line
Oakville, Ontario
L6M 3M9 Canada
(905) 825-0918
p. 92 (left)

Paul Warchol
Paul Warchol Photography, Inc.
224 Centre Street, 5th fl.
New York, NY 10013
(212) 431-3461
p. 92 (right)

Photo Credits

The New
Flooring Idea Book

Creating Style from the Ground Up

Dennis Jenkins
Dennis Jenkins and Associates Interior Design
5813 South West 68th Street
Miami, FL 33143
(305) 665-6960
pp. 108–111

Ted Montgomery
Indiana Architecture and Design
477 Ten Stones Circle
Charlotte, Vermont 05445
(802) 425-7717
www.indiana-architecture.com
Specialties: Sustainability, solar energy,
intentional communities.
pp. 116–121

Dalia Berlin, ASID
3511 Greenleaf Circle
Hollywood, FL 33021
(954) 967-6576
pp. 122–125

Leonard A. Hall
Endurance Flooring Co., Inc.
18460 NE 2nd Ave.
Miami, FL 33179
pp. 122–125

Alan Vaughn
Alan Vaughn Studios
3961 N. Ivy Road, NE
Atlanta, GA 30342
(770) 457-0820
alanvaughn@mindspring.com
p. 79

Desiree Caskill, ASID
Casa Mia Design
P. O. Box 140817
Coral Gables, Florida 33114
(305) 569-0529
casa-mia@msn.com
pp. 112–115

Joanne Hurd Kitchen and Bath Design
862 Washington Street
Gloucester, MA 01930
(978) 283-5105
p. 59 (right)

Cushman and Beckstrom
P. O. Box 655
82 Park Street
Stowe, Vermont 05672
(802) 253-2169
Specialties: Architecture, Interiors, Planning
pp. 17, 31, 34, 48 (left)s

David Hill and Susan Fuller,
Contractors
RR #1 Box 65
Woodstock, VT 05071
(802) 457-3943
Fax: (802) 457-4117
p. 97 (top)

Peggy Gowan, AIA
Jonathan Baily Associates
Dallas, Texas
(469) 227-3900
Fax: (469) 227-3901
p. 21

Jeffrey Berkus, Architect
Santa Barbara, California
(805) 687-310
p. 23

Blackstock Leather
13452 Kennedy Road
Stouffville, L4A 7X5 Canada
(800) 663-6657
p. 91

Win Whittman, AIA
The Avatar Group
Austin, Texas
(512) 494-1548
p. 23

Scholz & Barclay, Architects
pp. 16, 77 (left)

Drysdale Associates Interior Design
pp. 25, 77 (right)

Rick Burt, Architect
pp. 45 (bottom right), 95

Scogin, Elam and Bray, Architects
pp. 45 (middle), 97 (bottom)

Berhard & Priestly, Architects
p. 71 (top right)

Reiter & Reiter, Architects
p. 45 (top left)

Tom Rouselle, Architect
p. 71 (bottom right)

Lo Yi Chan, Architect
p. 94 (top left)

Stephen Blatt Architects
p. 94 (bottom left)

Tom Catalano, Architect
p. 94 (bottom right)

Rob Whitten, Architect
p. 98 (top)

Ann Sacks
8120 NE 33rd Drive
Portland, OR 97211
(800) 278-8453
www.annsacks.com
p. 66, 67 (bottom), 103 (top left), 105, 106, 107

Alan Vaughn
Alan Vaughn Studios
3961 North Ivy Road, NE
Atlanta, GA 30342
(770) 457-0820
p. 79

Walker Zanger
13190 Telfair Ave.
Sylmar, CA 91342
(818) 504-0235
pp. 57, 65, 67 (top)

Harris-Tarkett, Inc.
P. O. Box 300
Johnson City, TN 37605
(423) 928-3122
pp. 33, 37 (top left),
49 (bottom)

Michaelian & Kohlberg
578 Broadway, 2nd Fl.
New York, NY 10012
(212) 431-9009
p. 62, 63 (right)

Kentucky Wood Floors, Inc.
4200 Reservoir Ave.
Louisville, KY 40213
(502) 451-6024
p. 75

Country Floors
8735 Melrose Ave.
Los Angeles, CA 90069
(213) 657-0510
p. 81 (top left)

Mafi Wide Plank Flooring
Schneegattern, Austria
in U.S.A.: (804) 754-7181
p. 73 (top left)

Design Credits

A & M Wood Specialty
358 Eagle Street N.
Cambridge, ON N3H 5M2
(800) 265-2759
www.amwoodinc.com

A. E. Sampson & Son
P. O. Box 1010,
171 Camden Road
Warren, ME 04864
Phone: (207) 273-4000
Fax: (207) 273-4006
ddlewis@msn.com

ADI Corp.
5000 Nicholson Court
Bethesda, MD 20895
Phone: (301) 468-6856
Fax: (301) 468-0562
Marble and granite flooring

Aged Woods
147 West Philadelphia Street
York, PA 17403
Phone: (800) 233-9307
Fax: (717) 843-8104

Albany Woodworks
P. O. Box 729
Albany, LA 70711-0729
Phone: (225) 567-1155
Fax: (225) 567-5150
www.albanywoodworks.com

American Olean Tile Company
Box 271
Lansdale, PA 19446-0271
(215) 855-1111

American Rug Craftsmen
3090 Sugar Valley Rd. N.W.
Sugar Valley, GA 30746-5166
(800)-553-1734

AMS Imports Area Rugs
23 Ash Lane
Amherst, MA 01002
Phone: (800) 648-1816
Fax: (413) 256-0434
www.amsimports.com

Anderson Hardwood Floors
P. O. Box 1155
Clinton, SC 29325
Phone: (864) 833-6250
Fax: (864) 833-6664
www.andersonfloors.com

Ann Sacks
8120 NE Thirty-Third Drive
Portland, OR 97211
Phone: (503) 281-7751
Fax: (503) 287-8807
www.annsacks.com

Antiquarian Traders
9031 W. Olympic Boulevard
Beverly Hills, CA 90211-3541
Phone: (310) 247-3900
Fax: (310) 247-8864
www.antiquariantraders.com

Antique Woods and Colonial Restorations
1273 Reading Avenue
Boyertown, PA 19512
Phone: (888) 261-4284
www.vintagewoods.com

Architectural Timber & Millwork
49 Mount Warner Road
Hadley, MA 01035-0719
Phone: (413) 586-3045
Fax: (413) 586-3046

Armstrong World Industries
P. O. Box 3001
Lancaster, PA 17604
Phone: (717) 397-0611

ArtWorks Studio
337 Hayhne Ave. S.W.
Aiken, SC 29801
Phone: (803) 643-8335
Fax: (803) 643-8335
Floorcloths

Asia Minor Carpets
236 Fifth Avenue, 2nd Fl.
New York, NY 10001
Phone: (212) 447-9066
Fax: (212) 447-1879
Atlanta Oriental Rug Restoration
131 Bradford Street N.W.
Gainesville, GA 30501
Phone: (800) 926-7847
Fax: (770) 536-2228
rugray@mindspring.com

Augusta Lumber Co.
567 N. Charlotte Avenue
Waynesboro, VA 22980
Phone: (540) 946-9150
Fax: (540) 946-9168
www.comclin.net/augustalumber

Authentic Pine Floors
4042 Highway 42,
P. O. Box 206
Locust Grove, GA 30248
(770) 957-6-38
www.authenticpinefloors.com

Authentic Wood Floors
P. O. Box 153
Glen Rock, PA 17327
Phone: (717) 428-0904
Fax: (717) 428-0464

Award Hardwood Floors
401 N. 72nd Avenue
Wausau, WI 54401
Phone: (715) 849-8080
Fax: (715) 849-8081

Azrock Commercial Flooring
P. O. Box 354
Florence, AL 35631-0354
Phone: (800) 877-8455
Fax: (256) 766-3381
www.domco.com
A Division of Domco Inc.

Bamboo Flooring International
20950 Currier Road
Walnut, CA 91789
Phone: (800) 827-9261
Fax: (909) 594-6938
www.bamboo-flooring.com

Bangor Cork Company
William and D Street
Pen Argyl, PA 18072
(215) 863-9041

Barn Stormers
RR 1, Box 566
West Lebanon, ME 04027
(207) 658-9000

Barnes Lumber Manufacturing
P. O. Box 1383
Statesboro, GA 30459
Phone: (912) 768-8875
Fax: (912) 764-8713
www.barneslumber.com

Birger Juell, Ltd.
1337 Merchandise Mart
Chicago, IL 60654
Phone: (312) 464-9663
Fax: (312) 464-9664
Wood floors

Bloomsburg Carpet Industries
919 Third Avenue
New York, NY 10022
(212) 688-7447

BM Barnsiding
562 Rt. 17M
Monroe, NY 10950
Phone: (800) 499-0444
Fax: (914) 783-9471
bmbarn@frontiernet.net

Braid-Aid
466 Washington Street
Pembroke, MA 02359
(617) 826-6091

Brintons Carpets (USA) Limited
E-240 Route 4
Paramus, NJ 07652
(201) 368-0080

Broad-Axe Beam Co.
1320 Lee Roadz
Guilford, VT
Phone: (802) 257-0064
Fax: (802) 257-0064

Bruce Hardwood Floors
16803 Dallas Parkway
Addison, TX 75001
Phone: (800) 722-4647
Fax: (214) 887-2234
www.brucehardwoodfloors.com

Buckingham-Virginia Slate Corp.
P. O. Box 8
Arvonia, VA 23004-0008
Phone: (804) 581-1131
Fax: (804) 581-1130

Carlisle Restoration Lumber
1676 Route 9
Stoddard, NH 03464
Phone: (800) 595-9663
Fax: (603) 446-3540
www.wideplankflooring.com

Carpet and Rug Institute
P. O. Box 2048
Dalton, GA 30722-2048
Phone: (800) 882-8846
Fax: (706) 278-8835
www.carpet-rug.com

Centre Mills Antique Floors
P. O. Box 16
Aspers, PA 17304
Phone: (717) 334-0249
Fax: (717) 334-6223
www.igateway.com/mall/homeimp/wood/index

Charles R. Stock/V'Soske.
2400 Market Street
Philadelphia, PA 19103
(215) 568-3448
Carpets

Chestnut Specialists, Inc.
400 Harwinton Avenue
Plymouth, CT 06782
Phone: (860) 283-4209
Fax: (860) 283-4209
www.chestnutspec.com

Resources

Chestnut Woodworking & Antique Flooring Co.
P. O. Box 204
West Cornwall, CT 06796
Phone: (860) 672-4300
Fax: (860) 672-2441
www.chestnutwoodworking.com

Classic Revivals
1 Design Centter Place, Suite 545
Boston, MA 02210
Phone: (617) 574-9030
Fax: (617) 574-9027
Carpets

Columbia Forest Products
222 S.W. Columbia Street, Suite 1575
Portland, OR 97201-1575
Phone: (800) 547-4261
Fax: (503) 224-5294
www.columbiaproducts.com

Columbia Trading Company
547 S.W. Gaines Street
Portland, OR 97201
Phone: (888) 326-3477
Fax: (503) 279-8793
www.oregonlive.com/sites/columbiatrading

Congoleum Corporation
3705 Quakerbridge Road
P. O. Box 3172
Mercerville, NJ 08619-0127
Phone: (609) 584-3000
Fax: (609) 584-3518
www.congoleum.com

Conklin's Authentic Antique Barnwood &
Hand Hewn Beams
RD 1, Box 70
Butterfield Road
Susquehanna, PA 18847
Phone: (570) 465-3832
Fax: (570) 465-3835
www.conklinsbarnwood.com

Cordts Flooring Company
840 Lyle Court
Peekskill, NY 10566
Phone: (914) 737-8201
Fax: (914) 737-8201

Cork America
5657 Santa Monica Boulevard
Los Angeles, CA 90038
Phone: (213) 469-3228
Fax: (213) 465-5866

Costikyan Carpets
28-13 14th Street
Long Island City, NY 11102
(800) 247-7847

Cottage Interiors
396 Main St.
Bar Harbor, ME 04609-1511
Phone: (207) 288-5614
Fax: (207) 288-5421
www.cottageinteriors.com
Rugs

Country Braid House
462 Main St.
Tilton, NH 03276
Phone: (603) 286-4511
Fax: (603) 286-4155
www.countrybraidhouse.com

Country Floors, Inc.
15 East 16th Street
New York, NY 10003
(212) 627-8300

Country Settings
3305 W. Fourth Avenue
Belle, WV 25015
Phone: (304) 925-3863
Fax: (304) 925-3303
www.countrysettings.com

Country Wood Products
656 Fourth Street
Audubon, MN 56511
Phone: (218) 439-3385
Fax: (218) 439-3771

Couristan
919 Third Avenue
New York, NY 10022
(212) 371-4200

CPN
705 Moore Station Industrial Park
Prospect Park, PA 19076
Phone: (800) 437-3233
Fax: (610) 534-2285
www.cpninc.com
Underlayments, radiant heat

Craft House Inn Design Studio
S. England Street
Williamsburg, VA 23187
Phone: (757) 220-7503
Fax: (757) 221-8790

Craftsman Lumber Company
436 Main Street
Groton, MA 01450-0222
Phone: (978) 448-5621
Fax: (978) 448-2754
www.craftsmanlumber.com

Craftsman Style
1453 Fourth Street
Santa Monica, CA 90401
Phone: (310) 393-1468
Fax: (310) 393-5359
Carpets

Creative Tile Marketing
12323 S.W. 55th Street
Building 1000, Suite 1009-1010
Fort Lauderdale, FL 33330
Phone: (305) 858-8242
Fax: (305) 858-9926

Crossville Ceramics Co.
P. O. Box 1168
Crossville, TN 38557
Phone: (931) 484-2110
Fax: (931) 484-8418
www.crossville-ceramics.com

Daltile
7834 Hawn Freeway
P. O. Box 170130
Dallas, TX 75217
Phone: (800) 933-8453
Fax: (214) 309-4457
www.daltile.com

Design Materials
241 S. 55th St.
Kansas City, KS 66106
Phone: (913) 342-9796
Fax: (913) 342-9826
Natural fiber floor coverings

Designs in Tile
P. O. Box 358
Mount Shasta, CA 96067
Phone: (530) 926-2629
Fax: (530) 926-6467
www.designsintile.com

DLW Flooring Systems
Represented by Anderson, Dewald and
Associates
2750 Northaven, Suite 120
Dallas, TX 75229
(414) 247-4955
Linoleum

Domko Inc.
1001 Yamaska, Dept. TH1197
E. Farnham, Quebec J2N-1J7
(514) 293-3173

Duluth Timber Company
P. O. Box 16717
Duluth, MN 55816
Phone: (218) 727-2145
Fax: (218) 727-0393
www.duluthtimber.com

Dynamic Laser Applications
4704 Ecton Drive
Marietta, GA 30066
Phone: (770) 924-4998
Fax: (770) 926-5122

Eaton Hill Textile Works
334 Jake Martin Rd.
Marshfield, VT 05658
(802) 426-3733
ktsmith@connriver.net

Echeguren Slate
1495 Illinois Street
San Francisco, CA 94107
Phone: (800) 992-0701
Fax: (415) 206-9353
www.echeguren.com

Edward Molina Designs
196 Selleck Street
Stamford, CT 06902
(203) 967-9445
Carpets

Endicott Clay Products
Box 17
Fairbury, NE 68352
Phone: (402) 729-3315
Fax: (402) 729-5804

Environmental Design
908 S. E. 15th Street
Forest Lake, MN 55025
Phone: (612) 464-6190
Fax: (612) 464-6191

Epro, Inc.
156 E. Broadway
Westerville, OH 43081
Phone: (614) 882-6990
Fax: (614) 882-4210
One-of-a-kind ceramic tile

Esquire Ceramic Tile
300 International Boulevard
Clarksville, TN 37040
Phone: (800) 256-7924
Fax: (931) 647-9934
esquire@gish.com

European Treasures
72 N. Main Street
Hudson, OH 44236
(216) 656-4390

Family Heirloom Weavers
775 Meadowview Drive
Red Lion, PA 17356
Phone: (717) 246-2431
Fax: (717) 246-7439
www.familyheirloomweavers.com
Firebird Industries Ltd.
366 Hord Street
New Orleans, LA 70123
Phone: (504) 733-8204
Fax: (504) 733-8261
Ceramic tile

Floor Cloths of Arizona
527 W. Lawrence Lane
Phoenix, AZ 85021
(602) 371-9300
www.floorclothsofarizona.com

Resources

Florida Tile Industries
P. O. Box 447
Lakeland, FL 33802
Phone: (941) 687-7171
Fax: (941) 284-4007
www.fltile.com

Forbo Industries
Maplewood Drive
Hazelton, PA 18201
Phone: (800) 342-0604
Fax: (570) 450-0258
www.forbo-industries.com

Fulper Tile
34 W. Ferry Street
New Hope. PA 19067
Phone: (215) 862-3358
Fax: (215) 862-1318
fulpertile@aol.com

Good and Company
Salzburg Square, Route 101
Amherst, NH 03031
(603) 672-0490
Floorcloths

Goodwin Heart Pine Company
106 S.W. 109th Place
Micanopy, FL 32667
Phone: (352) 466-0339
Fax: (352) 466-0608
www.heartpine.com
goodwin@heartpine.com

Grigsby/Hallman Studio
1322 West Broad Street
Richmond, VA 23220
(804) 353-3738
Floorcloths, stenciling

Grill Works
1609 Halbur Road
Marshall, MN 56258
Phone: (800) 347-4745
Fax: (507) 532-3526
www.grillworks.com
Hardwood registers

H.K. Hardwoods
195 Libert Street
Brockton, MA 02401
Phone: (800) 530-0622
Fax: (508) 588-4698

Handwoven
6818 54th Avenue, N.E.
Seattle, WA 98115
(206) 524-9058
Rag rugs

Hardwood Council
P. O. Box 525
Oakmont, PA 15139
(412) 281-4980

Hardwood Information Center
100 First Avenue, Suite 525
Pittsburgh, PA 15222
Phone: (412) 323-9320
Fax: (412) 323-9334
www.hardwood.org

Harris-Tarkett
2225 Eddie Williams Road
Johnson City, TN 37601-2872
Phone: (423) 928-3122
Fax: (423) 928-9445
www.harristarkett.com
Solid, engineered, and laminate wood
flooring

Hartco Wood Flooring
565 Hartco Drive
Oneida, NY 37841
Phone: (800) 442-7826
Fax: (423) 569-9031
www.hartcoflooring.com

Heartwood Lumber Company
5801 Rhodes Avenue
New Orleans, LA 70131
Phone: (504) 394-6925
Fax: (504) 394-3013

Heirloom Rugs
28 Harlem Street
Rumford, RI 02916
(401) 438-5672

Heritage Rugs
R.D.1, Box 404
Lahaska, PA 18931
(215) 794-7229
Rag rugs

Hilltop Slate
P. O. Box 201, Rte. 22A
Middle Granville, NY 12849
(518) 642-1220

Historic Floors of Oshkosh
911 East Main Street
Winneconne, WI 54986
Phone: (920) 582-9977
Fax: (920) 582-9971
info@historicfloors.com

Historical Hand Painted Tile
2104 E. Seventh Avenue
Tampa, FL 33605
Phone: (813) 247-6817
Fax: (813) 242-8021

Hoboken Floors
70 Demarest Drive
Wayne, NJ
(800) 222-1068

Dimension Lumber & Milling
517 Stagg Street
Brooklyn, NY 11237
Phone: (718) 497-1680
Fax: (718) 366-6531

Intarsia, Inc.
1851 Cypress Lake Drive, Suite B
Orlando, FL 32837
Phone: (407) 859-5800
Fax: (407) 859-7555

Interceramic, USA
2333 S. Jupiter Road
Garland, TX 75041
Phone: (800) 496-8453
Fax: (214) 503-5575
www.interceramicsusa.com

Interior Vision in the Craftsman Style
P. O. Box 867
Port Townsend, WA 98368
Phone: (888) 385-3161
Fax: (360) 385-4874

International Floors of America, Inc.
3355 Lenox Road, N.E., Suite 270
Atlanta, GA 30326
Phone: (404) 846-1112
Fax: (404) 846-1114
Centiva@aol.com

International Hardwood Flooring
7400 Edmund Street
Philadelphia, PA 19136
Phone: (800) 338-7481
Fax: (215) 624-4577

Isabel O'Neil Studio and Foundation
177 East 87th Street
New York, NY 10022
(212) 751-6414
Floorcloths, stenciling

J. L. Powell & Co
600 S. Madison Street
Whiteville, NC 28472
Phone: (800) 227-2007
Fax: (919) 642-3164

J.R. Burrows and Company
P. O. Box 522
Rockland, MA 02370
Phone: (781) 982-1812
Fax: (781) 982-1636
www.burrows.com
merchant@burrows.com
carpets

Janos P. Spitzer Flooring Company
44 West 22nd Street
New York, NY 10010
(212) 627-1818

John Sherman
P. O. Box 152
West Pawlet, VT 05775
(802) 645-9828
Floorcloths

Kahrs International Inc.
951 Mariners Island Boulevard
San Mateo, CA 94404
(800) 800-5247
www.kahrs.com

Karastan Bigelow
P. O. Box 3089
Greenville, SC 29602
(803) 299-2000

Kentile Floors
58 Second Avenue
New York, NY 11215
(718) 768-9500

Kentucky Wood Floors
P. O. Box 33276
Louisville, KY 40232
Phone: (800) 235-5235
Fax: (502) 451-6027
www.kentuckywood.com

Kitchens Unique, Inc. by Lois
P. O. Box 689
259 Main St.
Chester, NJ 07930
Phone: (908) 879-6473
Fax: (908) 879-2446

L'esperance Tileworks
240 Sheridan Avenue
Albany, NY 12210
(518) 465-5586

Lacey-Champion Carpets
Box 216
Fairmount, GA 30139
(404) 337-5355

Langhorne Carpet Co.
P. O. Box 7175
201 W. Lincoln Highway
Penndel, PA 19047-0824
Phone: (215) 757-5155
Fax: (215) 757-2212

Launstein Hardwood Products
384 Every Road
Mason, MI 48854
Phone: (517) 676-1133
Fax: (517) 676-6379

Resources

Liberty Cedar
535 Libert Lane
West Kingston, RI 02892
Phone: (800) 882-3327
Fax: (401) 789-0320
lc@libert-cedar.com

Linden Lumber
P. O. Drawer 480369
Highway 43N
Linden, AL 36748
Phone: (334) 295-8751
Fax: (334) 295-8088

Linoleum City
5657 Santa Monica Boulevard
Hollywood, CA 90038
(213) 469-0063

Lizzie and Charlie's Rag Rugs
210 E. Bullion Avenue
Marysvale, UT 84750
(801) 326-4213
www.marysvale.org

London Tile Co.
65 Walnut Street
New London, OH 44851
Phone: (888) 757-1551
Fax: (419) 929-1552

Longwood Restoration
330 Midland Place
Lexington, KY 40505
Phone: (800) 225-7857
Fax: (606) 299-8205

M. L. Condon Company
254 Ferris Avenue
White Plains, NY 10603
Phone: (914) 946-4111
Fax: (914) 946-3779
Lumber and millwork

Manhattan Art & Antiques Center
1050 Second Avenue
New York, NY 10022
Phone: (212) 355-4400
Fax: (212) 355-4403
www.the_maac.com

Mannington
P. O. Box 30, Route 45
Salem, NJ 08079-0030
Phone: (856) 935-3000
Fax: (856) 339-5948
www.mannington.com

Marblelife
805 W. N. Carrier Parkway
Suite 220
Grand Prairie, TX 75050
Phone: (800) 627-4569
Fax: (972) 623-0220
www.marblelife.com

Mark Inc.
323 Railroad Avenue
Greenwich, CT 06830
Phone: (800) 227-0927
Fax: (203) 861-0197
Carpets

Marlborough Country Barn
N. Main Street
Marlborough, CT 06447
Phone: (800) 852-8893
Fax: (860) 295-7424
Rugs

Mary Moross Studios
122 Chambers Street
New York, NY 10007
Phone: (212) 571-0437
Fax: (212) 267-6594
Floorcloths

Mcintyre Tile Co.
55 W. Grantt Street
Healdsburg, CA 95448
Phone: (707) 433-8866
Fax: (707) 433-0548
www.mcintyre-tile.com

Mexican Handcrafted Tile/MC Designs
7595 Carroll Rd.
San Diego, CA 92121
Phone: (858) 689-9596
Fax: (858) 689-9597

Michael FitzSimmons Decorative Arts
311 W. Superior Street
Chicago, IL 60610
Phone: (312) 787-0496
Fax: (312) 787-6343

Michaelian & Kohlberg
578 Broadway, 2nd Fl.
New York, NY 10012
Phone: (212) 431-9009
Fax: (212) 431-9077
Carpets

Milliken Contract Carpeting
P. O. Box 2956
La Grange, GA 30241
(404) 883-5511

Milton W. Bosley Co.
P. O. Box 576
Glen Burnie, MD 21061
Phone: (800) 638-5010
Fax: (410) 553-1575
mbosley@clark.net
Wood moldings

Mintec Corp.
100 E. Pennsylvania Avenue, Suite 210
Towson, MD 21286
Phone: (888) 9-MINTEC
Fax: (410) 296-6693
www.bamtex.com
Bamboo flooring

Moravian Pottery and Tile Works
Swamp Road
Doylestown, PA 18901
(215) 345-6722

Mountain Lumber
P. O. Box 289
Ruckersville, VA 22968
(800) 445-2671
www.mountainlumber.com

Nature's Loom
32 E. 31st Street
New York, NY 10016
Phone: (800) 365-2002
Fax: (212) 213-8414
www.naturesloom.com

New England Hardwood Supply Co. Inc.
100 Taylor Street
Littleton, MA 01460
Phone: (800) 540-8683
Fax: (978) 486-9703

New England Wholesale Hardwoods
Rt. 82 S, Box 534
Pine Plains, NY 12567-0534
Phone: (518) 398-9663
Fax: (518) 398-9666
www.floorings.com

NOFMA
P. O. Box 3009
Memphis, TN 38173
Phone: (901) 526-5016
Fax: (901) 526-7022
www.nofma.org
Trade organization for hardwood flooring
manufacturers

Nordic American Corp.
15 Plantation Drive
Atlanta, GA 30324
Phone: (800) 242-8160
Fax: (404) 250-9531
Engineered flooring

North American Slate
50 Columbus St.
Granville, NY 12832
Phone: (518) 642-1702
Fax: (518) 642-3255
nas99slate@aol.com

Old World Restorations
7901 Thayer Drive
Fort Smith, AR 72908
(501) 646-1328
Slate floor repair

Ould Colony Artisans
169 Albert Ave.
Cranston, RI 02905-3811
Phone: (800) 414-7906
Fax: (401) 781-0775
Floorcloths

Paris Ceramics (USA) Inc.
151 Greenwich Avenue
Greenwich, CT 06830
Phone: (203) 552-9658
Fax: (203) 552-9655

Parquet de France
54 Byram Road
Point Pleasant, PA 18950-0156
Phone: (215) 297-5255
Fax: (215) 297-5255
Importers of French parquet

Past Perfect
1212 Washington Street
Holliston, MA 01746
Phone: (508) 429-7752
Fax: (508) 429-5997
viatorcomm@aol.com
Floorcloths

Patina Woods Company
3563 New Franklin Road
Chambersburg, PA 17201
(717) 264-8009

Patterson, Flynn & Martin
979 Third Avenue
New York, NY 10022
Phone: (212) 688-7700
Fax: (212) 826-6740
Rugs and carpeting

PED Products Company
P. O. Box 321
Springfield, PA 19064
(215) 328-4950
Linoleum

Peerless Imported Rugs
3028 North Lincoln Avenue
Chicago, IL 60657
(800) 621-6573

Pennsylvannia Woven Carpet Mills
401 East Allegheney Avenue
Philadelphia, PA 19134
(610) 215-5833

Resources

Pergo/ Perstop Flooring, Inc.
P. O. Box 1775
Horsham, PA 19044
(800) 337-3746
www.pergo.com

Persnickety
P. O. Box 458
776 East Walker Road
Great Falls, VA 22066
(703) 450-7150
Rag and hooked rugs

Pewabic Pottery
10125 E. Jefferrson Avenue
Detroit, MI 48214
Phone: (313) 822-0954
Fax: (313) 822-6266
www.pewabic.com

Piedmont Hardwood Flooring
P. O. Box 3070
Macon, GA 31205
Phone: (888) 791-0155
Fax: (912) 781-7288

Plaza Hardwood
219 W. Manhattan Avenue
Santa Fe, NM 87501
Phone: (800) 662-6306
Fax: (505) 992-8766
www.plzfloor.com

Premier Wood Floors
16803 Dallas Parkway
Dallas, TX 75248
(800) 588-1707

Premium Hardwood Floors & Supplies Inc.
121 31st Street (corner of 3rd Avenue)
Brooklyn, NY 11232
Phone: (718) 369-3141
Fax: (718) 369-3139
www.premium-floors.com/pwf
pwf@premium-floors.com

Quality Woods
95 Bartley Road
Flanders, NJ 07034
Phone: (973) 584-7554
Fax: (973) 584-3875
teakwood1@sprynet.com

Rare Earth Hardwoods
6778 E. Traverse Highway
Traverse City, MI 49684
Phone: (800) 968-0074
Fax: (800) 968-0094

Rastetter Woolen Mill
5802 State Route 39
Millersburg, OH 44654
(216) 674-2103

Renaissance Tile & Marble
P. O. Box 412
Cherry Valley, NY 13320
Phone: (607) 264-8474
Fax: (607) 264-8474
www.tilemarbleandgranite.com

Riley Design
P. O. Box 626
Croton Falls, NY 10519-0626
(914) 277-0860
Floorcloths

Robbins Brothers
919 Third Avenue
New York, NY 10022
(212) 421-1050
Carpets

Robbins Hardwood Flooring
4785 Eastern Avenue
Cincinnati, OH 45226
(800) 733-3309
www.robbinsflooring.com

Rosecore Carpets
979 Third Avenue
New York, NY 10022
(212) 421-7272

Rustigian Rugs
1 Governor Street
Providence, RI 02906
(401) 751-5100

Sandy Pond Hardwoods
921-A Lancaster Pike
Quarryville, PA 17566
Phone: (800) 546-9663
Fax: (717) 284-5739
www.figuredhardwoods.com

Saxony Carpet Company
979 Third Avenue
New York, NY 10022
(212) 755-7100

Scalamandre
950 Third Avenue
New York, NY 10022
(212) 980-3888
Carpets

Schumacher
79 Madison Avenue
New York, NY 10016
(800) 332-3384
Carpets

Schumacher and Company
938 Third Avenue
New York, NY 10022
(212) 415-3900

Seneca Tiles
7100 S. Country Road, Suite 23
Attica, OH 44807
Phone: (800) 426-4335
Fax: (419) 426-1735

Shaw Rugs
P. O. Drawer 2128
Dalton, GA 30722-2128
(800) 282-SHAW

Sheldon Slate Products Co. Inc.
Fox Road
Middle Granville, NY 12849
Phone: (518) 642-1280
Fax: (518) 642-9085
www.sheldonslate.com

Shep Brown Associates
24 Cummings Park
Woburn, MA 01801
Phone: (617) 935-8080
Fax: (617) 935-2090
www.shepbrownassociates.com
Tile and stone

Smith & Fong
650-872-1184
Plyboo

Southeastern Lumber Manufacturers
Association
P. O. Box 1788
Forest Park, GA 30051-1788
Phone: (404) 361-1445
Fax: (404) 361-5963

Special Effects by Sue
8113 Oakbrook Lane, S.W.
Tacoma, WA 98498
(206) 582-7821
Floorcloths

Stark Carpet
979 Third Avenue
New York, NY 10022
Phone: (212) 752-9000
Fax: (212) 758-4342
www.starkcarpet.com

Stone Tech
24-16 Queens Plaza S.
Long Island City, NY 11101
Phone: (718) 784-4646
Fax: (718) 784-1580
stonetech@aol.com

Structural Slate Co.
222 E. Main St.
P. O. Box 187
Pen Argyl, PA 18072
Phone: (800) 677-5283
Fax: (610) 863-7016
www.structuralslate.com

Sturbridge Yankee Workshop
Blueberry Road
Westbrook, ME 04092
Phone: (800) 343-1144

Summitville Tiles
P. O. Box 73
Summitville, OH 43962
Phone: (330) 223-1511
Fax: (330) 223-1414
www.summitville.com

Superior Water-Logged Lumber Co.
2200 E. Lake Shore Drive
Ashland, WI 54806
Phone: (715) 685-9663
Fax: (715) 685-9620
www.oldlogs.com

Sylvan Brandt
651 E. Main St.
Lititz, PA 17543
Phone: (717) 626-4520
Fax: (717) 626-5867
www.sylvanbrandt.com

Tarkett Inc.
1139 Lehigh Avenue
Whitehall, PA 18052
(800) 367-8275
www.tarkettna.com

Terra Designs
241 East Blackwell Street
Dover, NJ 07801
(201) 539-2999
Tile

Terrazzo & Marble Supply Companies
5700 S. Hamilton
Chicago, IL 60636
Phone: (773) 471-0700
Fax: (773) 471-5010

Resources

The Carpet and Rug Institute
P. O. Box 2048
Dalton, GA 30722
Phone: (800) 882-8846
Fax: (706) 278-8835

The Gazebo of New York
660 Madison Avenue
New York, NY 10021
(212) 832-7077
Rag, braided, and hooked rugs

The Joinery Company
P. O. Box 518
Tarboro, NC 27886
(252) 823-3306

The Persian Carpet
5634 Chapel Hill Boulevard
Durham, NC 27707
Phone: (800) 333-1801
Fax: (919) 439-3529

The Roof Tile & Slate Co.
1209 Carrol
Carollton, TX 75006
Phone: (800) 446-0220
Fax: (972) 242-1923
www.rts.com

The Woods Co.
5045 Kansas Avenue
Chambersburg, PA 17201
Phone: (717) 263-6524
Fax: (717) 263-9346

Thomas D. Osborn
1421 Northampton Street
Holyoke, MA 01040
Phone: (413) 532-9034
Fax: (413) 532-0241
Marquetry and inlaid floors

Tile Restoration Center
3511 Interkae Avenue N.
Seattle, WA 98103
Phone: (206) 633-4866
Fax: (206) 633-3489
www.tilerestorationcenter.com

Tile Showcase
291 Arsenal Street
Watertown, MA 02172
Phone: (617) 926-1100
Fax: (617) 926-9714

Tilecera
300 International Boulevard
Clarksville, TN 37040
Phone: (800) 782-8453
Fax: (931) 647-9934

U.S. Axminster
Box 877
East Union Extended
Greenville, MS 38702-0877
(601) 332-1581

U.S. Ceramic Tile Co.
10233 Sandyville Road, S.E.
East Sparta, OH 44626-9333
Phone: (330) 866-5531
Fax: (330) 866-5340
www.usceramictileco.com

Universal Flooring
14800 Quorum Drive, Suite110
(972) 387-0867
Dallas, TX 75240

Vermont Structural Slate Co.
P. O. Box 98
3 Prospect Street
Fair Haven, VT 05743
Phone: (800) 343-1900
Fax: (802) 265-3865

Vintage Lumber and Construction
Company
9507 Woodsboro Road
Frederick, MD 21701
(301) 898-7859

Vintage Pine
P. O. Box 85
Prospect, VA 23960
Phone: (804) 248-9000
Fax: (804) 248-9409

Walker Zanger
8901 Bradley Avenue
Sun Valley, CA 91352
Phone: (818) 504-0235
Fax: (818) 504-2226
Tile and stone

Wilsonart International
2400 Wilson Place
P. O. Box 6110
Temple, TX 76503-6110
Phone: (800) 710-8846
Fax: (817) 778-2711
www.wilsonart.com
Laminates

Winterthur Museum, Garden, and Library
Kennett Pike
Winterthur, DE 19810
Phone: (800) 448-3883
Fax: (302) 888-4820
Carpets

Woodawrd & Greenstein/Woodard Weave
506 E. 74th Street, 5th Fl.
New York, NY 10021
Phone: (800) 332-7847
Fax: (212) 734-9665
wgantiques@aol.com

Woodhouse
P. O. Box 7336
Rocky Mount, NC 27804
Phone: (919) 977-7336
Fax: (919) 641-4477

World Class Floors
333 S.E. Second Avenue, Suite 168
Portland, OR 97214
Phone: (800) 547-6634
Fax: (503) 736-2566
www.contactintl.com

Yankee Exotic Woods
P. O. Box 211
Cornish, NH 03746
Phone: (603) 675-6206
Fax: (603) 675-6306

Yankee Pride
29 Parkside Circle
Braintree, MA 02184
(800) 848-7610

Yield House
P. O. Box 2525
Conway, NH 03818-2525
Phone: (800) 659-0206
Fax: (603) 447-1717

Resources

Regina Cole

Regina Cole has written extensively on architecture, interior design, and the history of the American decorative arts in both books and magazines. She is an editor-at-large at *Old-House Interiors* magazine, where she was a founding editor and, for many years, senior editor. She often lectures on the subject of historic kitchen styles, with emphasis on their suitability for modern living.

Regina Cole also writes travel articles, political commentary, and poetry. She lives in Gloucester, Massachusetts.

About the Author